SIX EXISTENTIAL HEROES

SIX EXISTENTIAL HEROES

The Politics of Faith

LUCIO P. RUOTOLO

Harvard University Press Cambridge, Massachusetts 1973

TO M. HOLMES HARTSHORNE

Acknowledgments

In dedicating this book to M. Holmes Hartshorne of Colgate University I convey my deep appreciation to the teacher who introduced me to the thought of Søren Kierkegaard. I am also grateful for the influence of Kurt F. Reinhardt and Kurt Müller-Volmer of Stanford University on my study of Husserl and Heidegger. My thanks to Robert McAfee Brown for his generosity with books and advice on theological matters and to Edwin M. Good for his Old Testament exegesis, particularly in regard to *Go Down, Moses*.

Thanks to William Chace, J. Martin Evans, David Halliburton, Dale Harris, Stuart McLean, David Riggs, Fred Robinson, Lawrence Ryan, and Wilfred Stone whose valuable suggestions contributed to the completion of the book; and to the students of my seminar "The Existential Hero in Modern Literature," whose response to my ideas over the past six years has proved so helpful.

The editor of *Modern Language Quarterly* kindly gave permission to quote a portion of Chapter 2 that appeared originally under the title "*Brighton Rock's* Absurd Heroine," in that magazine (25 [December 1964], 425–433). Finally, I should like to thank the Department of English and the Dean of Humanities and Sciences at Stanford University for helping meet the expense of preparing the manuscript.

L. R.

Stanford, California, March 1971

Contents

SIX EXISTENTIAL HEROES

Introduction

Historical Faith

Mankind, it seems, has always been fascinated with the idea of making something out of nothing. From earliest philosophical debates on *creatio ex nihilo* to modern symposiums on human creativity, the appeal of an insubstantial starting point reflects man's inclination to seek an abstract basis for life above or beyond the realities of his own troubled history. While existentialism emerges as an assault upon this type of thinking,[1] the experience of nothingness animates almost every aspect of existential literature. In perhaps the most familiar example, Sartre's Roquentin discovers himself at that moment when the roots of a chestnut tree and the familiar objects of the park in which he is seated melt suddenly into amorphous irrelevance. It takes something to witness nothing; even "to imagine nothingness," the narrator of *Nausea* speculates, "you had to be there already."[2]

If Roquentin fails to become an existential hero, it is because he will not remain in a world "where knowledge but increases vertigo."[3] Instead he seeks a basis for personality outside Being[4] and time—from the perspective I will emphasize in this book, outside historical existence. Leaving an unenlightened bourgeoisie to face the worst, Roquentin chooses to quit the world, in his own words, "to drive existence out of me, to rid the passing moments of their fat, to twist them, dry them, purify myself, harden myself, to give back at last the sharp, precise sound of a saxophone note."[5] The reality of art, conveyed through the voice he hears singing "Some of These Days" on a scratched phonograph record, offers a means of transcending the naked contingency he witnesses at the heart of everyday life.

Despite his preference for a world of abstract categories where "circles and melodies retain their pure and rigid contours,"[6] Roquentin represents a type of alienated protagonist whose affirmation of subjectivity is often confused

1

with existential freedom. The fault is not altogether with those who misunderstand Sartre's early artistic intentions. Roquentin's acute sense of meaninglessness, Iris Murdoch writes, "makes him look with clairvoyant amazement upon the bourgeoisie, past and present, of the town where he is living . . . To be outside society," she concludes, "often appears to have for Sartre a positive value. Gauguin and Rimbaud are minor saints in the existentialist calendar for this reason."[7]

The type of outsider to whom she refers prizes an inner freedom which, we must presume, is its own foundation. Shunning intimacy as he shuns social involvement (Roquentin's "melody stays the same, young and firm, like a pitiless witness") this protagonist strives, whether passively introspective or aggressively demoniac, to guard an inherent and immutable inwardness from external qualification. Possessing Truth, he requires nothing more to complete him.

Like many other critics, Marxist Georg Lukács conceives of the existential protagonist almost exclusively in these ahistorical terms. His twofold description of the literary outsider in *The Meaning of Contemporary Realism* helps further to clarify the distinction I wish to make. It bears quoting in full: "First, the hero is strictly confined within the limits of his own experience. There is not for him—and apparently not for his creator—any pre-existent reality beyond his own self, acting upon him or being acted upon by him. Secondly, the hero himself is without personal history. He is 'thrown-into-the-world': meaninglessly, unfathomably. He does not develop through contact with the world; he neither forms nor is formed by it. The only 'development' in this literature is the gradual revelation of the human condition. Man is now what he has always been and always will be."[8] Ironically, Lukács's criteria highlight the change that occurs in Sartre's conception of heroism and, more important for our present purpose, the historicized faith I will emphasize in six markedly different existential protagonists.[9]

2

Introduction

When, some years later, Sartre draws his portrait of the anti-Semite, Roquentin's preference for hard
purity reappears in less attractive guise. Unable to live with
uncertainty, the anti-Semite projects and localizes impermanence in the Jew, then drives him out of the world. Opposing
experience—he is a man who "seeks only what he has already
found" and "becomes only what he already was"—his hatred of
the Jew is itself an abstraction, preceding, Sartre tells us, "the
facts that are supposed to call it forth."[10] How striking by
contrast are those qualities of good faith Sartre describes on
these same pages: groping painfully for truth, the anti-Semite's
counterpart "knows that his reasoning is no more than tenta-
tive, that other considerations may supervene to cast doubt
on it. He never sees very clearly where he is going; he is
'open'; he may even appear to be hesitant."[11] Risking what we
will come to understand more clearly as the experience of
"nothing" he learns to see the world as something other than
an extension of his own rational and psychic needs.

Aware that reality is always more than his grasp of
it presumes, this figure, like the six heroes I will discuss, is
led beyond self-worship toward a continually expanding
vision of self and of world. No abstraction, the catalyst for
this dynamic expansion of consciousness is paradoxically
"nothing." Subverting man's determination to objectify and
thereby to control experience, "nothing" allows Being room
in which to reveal itself in new and mysterious ways. Open
to "nothing," the hero's life emerges dialectically as "something evermore about to be."

At the end of *Invisible Man*, Ralph Ellison's black
narrator, aware of his own inclination to resist new experience,
affirms the principle of growth that defines his new maturity:
"the mind that has conceived a plan of living must never lose
sight of the chaos against which that pattern was conceived."
The difficult idea that every structure of consciousness is
dialectically part of that chaos which negates it strikes us with

full resonance in the writing of Martin Heidegger. "Only because Nothing is revealed in the very basis of our *Da-sein,*" he stated in his inaugural lecture at Freiburg, "is it possible for the utter strangeness of what-is to dawn on us." The famous philosopher of existence went on to emphasize the need of "letting oneself go into Nothing, that is to say, freeing oneself from the idols we all have and to which we are wont to go cringing."[12] Man's failure to free himself from idolatry is finally for Heidegger as for the heroes I examine a denial of his experiential being in time. Before we can understand the sense in which this hero affirms history, however, we must understand more fully the appeal of those abstractions that tempt him to transcend it.

Modern thought and literature abound with examples. In W. H. Auden's *For the Time Being,* Herod mimics his subjects' self-sustaining religiosity: "The God I want and intend to get must be someone I can recognize immediately without having to wait and see what he says or does. There must be nothing in the least extraordinary about him. Produce him at once, please. I'm sick of waiting." Reflecting those bourgeois values Auden's prose and poetry parodies so well, he asks God to remain the familiar projection of human vanity, the god of middle-class religion Freud recognized and named. "Be interesting and weak like us," Herod interposes ironically before the infant Christ, "and we will love you as we love ourselves."[13]

As an important part of the existentialist movement, Freud probed the motivation of all such acts of projected deification. Creating gods in his own image, man tends to identify reality with wish fulfillment. The relief of tension is accomplished at the expense of human relationships, or, to employ another Freudian idiom, at the expense of the reality principle.

Readers of Robert Browning will recall Porphyria's lover as a psychopath who kills her at the height of love-

making, at the instant when she gives herself to him "forever."
Sane enough to know that existence breeds infidelity, he seeks
to preserve this special moment from future tension. The
logical extension of an acquisitive, sexual love, his decision
to strangle his mistress reflects the human compulsion to
ensure that neither time nor experience trancends
wish fulfillment.

> At last I knew
> Porphyria worshipped me: surprise
> Made my heart swell, and still it grew
> While I debated what to do.
> That moment she was mine, mine, fair,
> Perfectly pure and good: I found
> A thing to do, and all her hair
> In one long yellow string I wound
> Three times her little throat around,
> And strangled her.

With the close of his monologue, the narrator, seated with
the corpse of Porphyria in his arms, waits in a posture of
immobility for that sanction his own will seems helpless to
provide.

> And all night long we have not stirred,
> And yet God has not said a word!

God's silence, however, may reveal more than the
narrator's inability to take responsibility for his murder of
Being and time. A madman can project the answer he requires
on God as well as on mistress. Porphyria's lover does not.
Looking beyond himself, perhaps in the last gesture of his
humanity, he still conceives of life in terms of the future and,
more important, in terms of relationship. From the perspective
of demoniac heroism this is an expression of bad faith. From
the existential perspective I seek to establish, it suggests the

narrator is still responsive, however weakly, to something other than his own solipsistic intentions.

The demoniac rebel, urging us to go wrong in our own way rather than to go right in someone else's, requires no sanction short of his own will to act. He remains by nature antisocial. Murray Krieger, developing a conception of the existential hero based largely on Raskolnikov's premise in *Crime and Punishment* that "all great men or even men a little out of the common . . . must from their very nature be criminals," suggests that such a protagonist maintains independence through an act of revenge directed against all ethical absolutes, which is to say, against every external demand that would reduce his subjectivity. "Hopelessly adrift from his or any other moorings, he can float into will-lessness and thus abdicate from tragic heroism, or he can surge toward the demoniac."[14]

Despite Krieger's fine analysis of demoniac existentialism we may well question whether such protagonists are ever free, short of self-destruction, of that external world they choose to abrogate. The anti-Semite requires the Jew in order to sustain his image of himself. With the death of the last Jew, his reason for existing ends. In terms of Browning's poem he finds nothing further "to do." Similarly, the professor in Joseph Conrad's *The Secret Agent*, raising his glass "to the destruction of what is," lives in counterpoint to those he victimizes; as Conrad finally describes his being, "he had no future." Unable to relax their grip (lest they "float into will-lessness") reality remains for such figures an abstract extension of their own static death wish.

Like King Lear on the heath my six heroes survive a world in which villains go unpunished and madmen lead the blind. Each witnesses through his separate environment the naked absurdity of being in the world, Clarissa Dalloway in an empty room of her fashionable London apartment, Isaac McCaslin in a wilderness that was once the Mississippi

Introduction

Delta. The classical and romantic hero can be said to rise above historical ambivalence, testifying on the one hand to the reality of universal virtue and on the other to uncompromised inwardness; these modern heroes allow neither thought nor passion to tease them out of existence. In that silent abyss at the core of daily life, a depth mysteriously impervious to human intention, they are apt to wonder with the poet "what rough beast, its hour come round at last, / Slouches towards Bethlehem to be born?" They endure such expectation, however, in the posture of faith. Facing "the utter strangeness of what is" these heroes find new life, as I have suggested, in relationship to phenomena they no longer necessarily understand and control.

The depth each confronts is not some special dimension of Being manifest through a mystical suspension of profane experience. The most fanciful intimations remain for him a part of that limited particularity he honors and celebrates. The existential hero can ask—Why not nothing?—because, like the Abraham of Kierkegaard's *Fear and Trembling*, he cares about "something." The fondest expectations of faith exist for him against a background of daily routine.

Asked by God to sacrifice ("murder") his only son Isaac, Abraham's absurd faith is earthly to the last. "He did not believe that some day he would be blessed in the beyond, but that he would be happy here in the world." What alarms the narrator, Johannes de Silentio, is that Abraham can give up everything, his son as well as his sense of God's justice, and yet still be ready, in the concreteness of his own history, to receive Isaac back again; "to be able to lose one's reason, and therefore the whole of finiteness of which reason is the broker, and then by virtue of the absurd to gain precisely the same finiteness—that appalls my soul."[15] Abraham, however, is great by virtue of that existential faith the narrator admittedly lacks. Unable to let himself go into "nothing"— "I cannot shut my eyes and plunge confidently into the

absurd, for me that is an impossibility"—Johannes reveals
his own unwillingness to experience the paradoxical relationship of Being and nothing. Choosing to be a lyrical narrator,
he stays outside the dialectic, the romantic spectator of a
faith he can at best describe.[16]

While the Continental romantic poet represented for
Kierkegaard the antithesis of existential faith, he might have
found a different orientation had he read more of the English
Romantics. This book is not the place to develop these important similarities. We should notice, however, that concepts
such as "wise passiveness" and "negative capability" may
convey a similar courage to face "nothing." Poets like Blake,
Wordsworth, and Keats, cultivating the virtue of "not having,"
urge us to resist that human proclivity by which the unknown
is reduced to paradigm. These writers, moreover, celebrate
with no less intensity the holiness of an experience that often
threatens the very language they employ to name it.

The appeal of silence and the tendency to associate
silence and holiness ("The holy time is quiet as a Nun /
Breathless with adoration") are continually misunderstood
by critics who apply solely positivistic criteria to the intention
of the romantic poets.[17] Although concern with nonverbal
experience would appear to involve their language in a *reductio
ad absurdum*, it may also reveal a growing sense that speech,
like the apprehension of being-in-the-world, points beyond
itself toward a common, numinous ground.[18] The experimental
inclination in Romantic literature grows, at least in part, from
the idea that literary form, as well as language, involves an
act of mediation and, consequently, that all structures of
thought, in an important respect, are distinct from the phenomenological sources that provoked them.

As I have tried to suggest, however, the significance
created once experience is structured reveals those historical
premises that underlie consciousness. The experience
of phenomena presupposes a particular human being, existing

at a certain time and in a certain place. Consequently, the existential formulation of depth, far from the static dogma of the human condition Lukács suggests, reflects continually that change implied in all dialectical views of history.

If Henry James was correct in attributing to the novelist an independence unknown in other genres, it should not surprise us to find the modern novel a particularly rich field for exploring these developing assumptions about man and his environment. The six novelists I consider in the following chapters, three English (Virginia Woolf, Graham Greene, William Golding) and three American (William Faulkner, Ralph Ellison, Bernard Malamud) represent the widest spectrum of existential intention in English fiction during the past fifty years. None have been directly influenced, so far as I know, by the philosophers of existence, nor for that matter, by one another. Their backgrounds, in addition, are dissimilar: male, female, black, white, urban, rural, Jewish, Protestant, Catholic, and agnostic, to mention a few of the more obvious distinctions. I make two suppositions: first, that the conception of the hero of all these writers reveals a historicized treatment of existential experience, and second, that the six novels, presented in chronological order, typify those changes in historical consciousness that have affected the treatment of existential heroism.

The first three novels offer as representative of the twenties and thirties a hero concerned less with public than with personal history. Clarissa's expanded vision of the world allows her to see others within the confines of that upper-class "party world" she has chosen through marriage. Her authenticity involves no leap from this station of life to some "better" or more socially "useful" vocation. She is at the close what she was at the beginning: "a perfect hostess"; Rose Wilson is bound by an economic and social bondage she never seriously questions. Her British working-class values remain a decisive part of the new life she discovers in the

course of her relationship with Pinkie; Isaac McCaslin's act of
passing on the hunting horn to his black descendant cannot
eradicate the centuries of white racism that have helped to
form his consciousness of others. Each of the three, however,
breaks new ground. They prepare us for more public acts
of self-extension that, if I am correct, will prove increasingly
to characterize the form of existentially oriented novels.
Heroes like Invisibile Man, Ralph, and Yakov Bok, while resigned to the tentativeness of all human knowledge, risk experience in more openly political terms. *The Fixer* typifies
the emergence of a hero no less "existential" by virtue of revolutionary protest.

"If we assume that abstract thought is the highest
manifestation of human activity," Kierkegaard wrote in explication of existential faith."it follows that philosophy and
the philosophers proudly desert existence, leaving the rest
of us to face the worst."[19] The hero I introduce develops
in relation to that world he seeks to remedy. His faith remains
historical unto death.

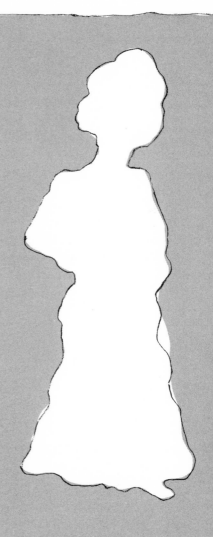

One October afternoon in 1929 Virginia Woolf was grasped by "inner loneliness" on the streets of London. Later that day, when considering this moment of "vacancy and silence," she recalled a similar emotion following her brother's death twenty years earlier. Her diary, however, reveals an important difference: "No one knows how I suffer, walking up this street, engaged with my anguish, as I was after Thoby died—alone; fighting something alone. But then I had the devil to fight, and now nothing." While failing to understand the disruptive feeling, she confesses that it has goaded her to reach beyond the habitable world. Virginia Woolf equates this "emptiness" with a new and no less obscure impression of freedom, "the sense that comes to me of being bound on an adventure; of being strangely free now, with money and so on, to do anything."[1]

A few months before her painful rejuvenation in the face of nothing, Martin Heidegger, appointed to the chair of philosophy at Freiburg, delivered his inaugural lecture on the primacy of such an experience. Heidegger's assertion that man must face nothing in order to be something, and Virginia Woolf's literary treatment of the dilemma she acknowledged in her own life, characterize the ontological reformation that with Schelling and Kierkegaard had begun to transform Western culture.[2]

The critical moment of absolute doubt, while symptomatic of the recurrent madness that plagued Virginia Woolf throughout her life, is a central concern of her most creative work. Rachel, the earliest of her heroines (*The Voyage Out*), is overcome by "the unspeakable queerness of the fact that she should be sitting in an arm-chair, in the morning, in the middle of the world" or "that things should exist at all." When Eleanor (*The Years*) questions her place in the world, she is gripped by the anxious sense of being "alone in the midst of nothingness." Louis (*The Waves*) directs his friends to the sound of the world "moving through abysses of infinite space," a blank and timeless reality that dissolves

identity. The theme is expressed in *Mrs. Dalloway* when
Septimus Smith, gazing at England from the window of a train,
ponders that "the world itself is without meaning."[3] Virginia
Woolf, in both critical essays and fiction, pictures man's acknowledgment of an absurd universe. Her chief artistic concern is to explore the nature of that intelligence capable of
surviving negation.

"Mr. Bennett and Mrs. Brown," a lecture she gave
at Cambridge in 1924 while working on *Mrs. Dalloway*,
raises the question of how and why a character appears real.
Woolf, like Heidegger, asks, What is Being?[4] Both novelist
and philosopher charge their contemporaries with uncritically
accepting society's concept of reality. Virginia Woolf speaks
of her age as defining "old women" through the predictable as-
sociations that make them discernible in the first place: "Old
women have houses. They have fathers. They have incomes.
They have servants. They have hot-water bottles. That is
how we know that they are old women."[5] She censures the
preceding Edwardians for their presumption that any sensible
man knows the difference between what is and what is not.
In her novels the heroes' function is to examine critically
the existential relevance of their own lives. Significantly,
meaning is revealed to these heroes when its antithesis becomes
more than a matter of sophistry. Her lecture, later published
in *The Captain's Death Bed*, offers "Mrs. Brown" as a touch-
stone for the virtue that is to characterize her most famous
protagonists.

Mrs. Brown is a fictitious name for an old woman
the lecturer once saw on a train to London. Virginia Woolf
recalls that as she sat opposite the stranger, Mrs. Brown was
in the midst of a serious talk with her companion, a stern-
faced man of about forty (he is given the effectively impersonal name of Smith); it was apparent to the intruder that the
latter had some power over the former "which he was exerting
disagreeably" (p. 99). Since they stopped their discussion in
her presence, she remains ignorant as to the cause of the

woman's suffering.

At first the novelist confesses the desire "like most people travelling with fellow passengers" somehow to account for them, and so she conceives the familiar details through which these unknown people might be established as more legible characters. The woman, she imagines, widowed years ago, has one son who is in some sort of trouble; her tormentor, dressed in good blue serge, is "very likely a respectable corn-chandler from the North" (p. 98).

When they begin speaking again, the small talk that Mr. Smith initiates with composed condescension verifies the power he holds over the little woman by his side. As the latter attempts to keep up the appearance of civility, resisting all of his menacing, though unspoken, demands, Virginia Woolf is suddenly aware of a superb dignity in Mrs. Brown's struggle to preserve the sanctity of her being against an overbearing and callous adversary: "She looked very small, very tenacious; at once very frail and very heroic." The lecturer recalls how at that moment a mysterious sense of Mrs. Brown's existence seemed to flow across the empty space of the compartment, disturbing her with an excitement that (like the experience of dread on the streets of London) she cannot fully understand. The impression the old lady made, Virginia Woolf tells us, "was overwhelming. It came pouring out like a draught, like a smell of burning" (pp. 100–101). All the facts packed into a three-volume novel of Mrs. Brown (and the traveler was tempted to write one) cannot improve upon this obscurely defined sense of recognition.

The Proustian manner in which Mrs. Brown's heroism appears to the novelist resists her effort to conceptualize the experience. Bothered by a sense of obscurity, Virginia Woolf turns to such eminent Edwardian novelists as H. G. Wells, John Galsworthy, and Arnold Bennett to study the way in which they communicated phenomena. Wells's utopian considerations, Galsworthy's social criticism, and Bennett's aesthetic predilection (she argues that Bennett tries

15

"to hypnotize us into the belief that, because he has made a house, there must be a person living there") presume the bond between reader and writer to be a common way of seeing and ordering experience, exemplified by the age's habit of describing old women. In each case it is not the particular existence of a Mrs. Brown that is the starting point for communication; rather, Virginia Woolf insists, these writers "were interested in something outside," and the nature of their respective ideologies determined their manner of seeing. For the Edwardian, essence preceded existence. Virginia Woolf suggests that her contemporaries have largely ignored the particularity of human existence: "With all his powers of observation, . . . Mr. Bennett has never once looked at Mrs. Brown in her corner" (p. 109).

Rather than censure the conventions which writers such as Arnold Bennett have utilized and developed, the novelist argues that changing times have rendered their ways obsolete: "For us those conventions are ruin, those tools are death" (p. 110). She seeks an idiom more in tune with the artistic and scientific break-throughs that have characterized the new century.

Mrs. Brown's presence dissipates the novelist's Edwardian frame of reference: "Details could wait. The important thing was to realize her character, to steep oneself in her atmosphere" (p. 101). The statement appears to assert the strange proposition that human personality is manifest in atmosphere rather than in substance. Virginia Woolf enunciates the emptiness that surrounds and separates people; space becomes her catalyst for communication. The idea is similar to Heidegger's formulation throughout *Being and Time* of that enveloping space within which "presence" is revealed.[6]

William Barrett, recalling Buber's I-Thou concept, suggests that "for Heidegger, the I can meet the Thou only because *There is*—i.e., can meet only within some encompassing region of Being. After all, I have to meet thee *somewhere*; in relation to something and in some context." Barrett considers the emphasis upon this "third presence," the region where subject and object can meet, as Heidegger's most important philosophical insight.[7]

Heidegger's concept of Being plunges all phenomenological experience into the uncertainty of a future that is yet to be and a past that is irredeemably over. The inauthentic man, unwilling to risk the void that borders meaning, maintains a static vision of existence. Only in nothingness, Heidegger stresses, lies the possibility for the emergence of a world that is more than the projection of derived intentions.

Utilizing her dramatic example, Virginia Woolf urges the modern writer to face a human dimension that both underlies and transcends "the fabric of things," to look beneath conventional behavior into a private world each of us possesses. The "world" she has in mind is radically different from that of her predecessors. It is a world in which impermanence and paradox ridicule bourgeois complacency, in which "you have gone to bed at night bewildered by the complexity of your feelings. In one day thousands of ideas have coursed through your brains; thousands of emotions have met, collided, and disappeared in astonishing disorder" (p. 118).

The threat of meaninglessness leads her to that same sense of creative possibility she was to describe in her diary. The old woman, existing in an atmosphere of "unlimited capacity and infinite variety," is free to say and do the unexpected. Everything about her, not least of all her silence, fascinates the writer for the reason expressed at the close of her essay: "She is, of course, the spirit we live by, life itself" (p. 119). The details of her face, her gestures, the quality of her speech, have emerged in a new light once the novelist has shared Mrs. Brown's crisis. Virginia Woolf's closing advice that English literature will reach a new greatness only "if we are determined never, never to desert Mrs. Brown"— like the axiom of phenomenology, *"Zu den Sachen selbst!"* ("To the things themselves!")—urges her contemporaries to tunnel with her into the depth of life and character, in search of what Husserl termed the "genesis of meaning" *(Sinngenesis)*.[8]

Mrs. Dalloway opposes the Edwardians' unwillingness to question their order; it also represents Virginia Woolf's effort to establish a perspective for the novel outside the realm of manners. The book, written several years before she recorded her suffering on the streets of London, like Heidegger's now classic study, explores nothingness within the context of Being and time.

Virginia Woolf in an early preface describes Septimus and Clarissa as doubles. Initially, the parallel seems obscure. Clarissa, a fashionable Edwardian matron, entrenched in the establishment of British society, lives within the bounds she has freely chosen. Above all she affirms with aristocratic fervor that particularly English virtue, the right to privacy. Septimus, returning from the war, a victim of shell shock (it is the summer of 1923), wanders with his Italian bride through an environment without form or function; only his consciousness qualifies absurdity. He likens himself to a half-drowned sailor, marooned on an uncharted rock in the midst of some nameless ocean. The novel pictures twelve hours in the lives of these two people, Clarissa preparing for one of her grand parties, Septimus in his private dialogue with cosmic anarchy. Although the two never meet, as the novelist develops her characters we realize they share a common insight through their experience of nothingness.

Clarissa's respect for the distance between human beings, more than a manifestation of detached decorum, leads her to defend Septimus' suicide when she hears of it late that evening. Her identification with Septimus is not a detail derived from those activities that describe Clarissa's life as a wealthy London matron. Indeed, the people closest to the heroine, bound by the conventions that define their social station, have the greatest difficulty perceiving her.

Mrs. Dalloway is more than casually concerned with the way in which people see. The world of Clarissa, her

double, and her former fiancé, Peter Walsh, takes on a novel
and frightening appearance once stripped of its predefined
context. "Things," Peter confesses after his disturbing interview with Clarissa, "stand out as if one had never seen them
before" (p. 107). Similarly, Peter's presence in her house
after years of absence makes Clarissa see herself in a new way.

Peter finds that the sight of her elicits an ambiguous
response. He is at once drawn to Clarissa as a reminder of
past affection and repulsed by the anxiety her presence occasions. When such encounters threaten his composure, he
seeks respite through the habit and affectation that predefine
him—the fondling of his penknife or his predictably romantic
invective against Edwardian decorum. Virginia Woolf stresses
Peter's compulsion for self-distraction during his fantasy
in the park, when, like the young Stephen Dedalus before the
Dublin prostitute, he urges the vision to grant him the peace
of non-being: "Let me walk straight on to this great figure,
who will, with a toss of her head, mount me on her streamers
and let me blow to nothingness with the rest" (p. 87).

The irony of the Edwardians' remedy for insanity
is implicit in Dr. Holmes's instructions for Septimus' wife to
force her husband to take notice of "real things." Each of
Rezia's pleas for Septimus to look at details elicits his despair
over the world that others would foist upon him: "But what
was there to look at?" (p. 37).

Rezia, we are told, could not help looking at detail.
When the motor car moves through the streets of London
arousing so much speculation as to the identity of the dignitary
behind the curtained window, her attention is riveted upon
the pattern of trees on the blinds. Like the silks and feathers
of the hats she manufactures, such details fully absorb her.
Dr. Holmes easily converts Rezia to the therapy of making
Septimus "take an interest in things outside himself" (p. 31).
His prescription typifies the inauthenticity that touches every
character in the novel. Rezia is forever concerned with
what other people will think of her husband's odd behavior.

Six Existential Heroes

Richard Dalloway is reminded that he loves his wife when he recalls that Peter Walsh once loved her. Clarissa gives parties so people will like her. About these central characters float a chorus of sleepwalkers, the countless passersby shaken into momentary consciousness by the backfiring of an automobile, merging with a crowd of onlookers before an airplane skywriting advertisements, seeking self-distraction in every object. Was the plane spelling toffee or soap? Was it the Prince of Wales or the Prime Minister whose face was seen in the passing car? What flowers to choose for the party? The man on the street, like Prufrock considering peaches and trouser cuffs, avoids the question that overwhelms Septimus.

Septimus' vision of the world alienates him from the objective order wife and psychiatrist urge him to emulate. Estranged from the sanity of others, "rooted to the pavement," the veteran asks "for what purpose" he is present. Virginia Woolf's novel honors and extends his question. He perceives a beauty in existence that his age has almost totally disregarded; his vision of new life—"Trees were alive" (p. 32)—is a source of joy as well as of madness. These obscure words, scribbled on pieces of paper, recall Wordsworth's critique of a world intent upon "getting and spending," out of touch with Being. Unfortunately, the glimpse of beauty that makes Septimus less forlorn is anathema to an age that worships like Septimus' inhuman doctor, Sir William Bradshaw, the twin goddesses "Proportion" and "Conversion" (pp. 150–151).

While the average inhabitant of London discourses on the commercial products advertised in the sky, Septimus is moved to tears by them: "the smoke words languishing and melting in the sky . . . one shape after another of unimaginable beauty" (p. 31). He participates in the presence of all he perceives (animate and inanimate alike). If the leaves themselves appear alive, they are connected "by millions of fibres with his own body" (p. 32), just as sparrows rising and falling between a host of objects are all part of the pattern.

"Sounds made harmonies with premeditation; the spaces between them were as significant as the sounds" (p. 33). Septimus, however, terrified by his eccentric vision, remains isolated from the everyday world.

Septimus and Clarissa realize detail each in a different way. When Septimus lies back in his chair, exhausted with fear, his body is suddenly thrilled by the sense of the earth beneath him. In exuberation he imagines that "red flowers grew through his flesh" (p. 103), their stiff leaves rustling by his head. During the fantasy, the flowers become roses that hang about him; it is only then that the vision reveals its source: his bedroom is wallpapered with thick red roses. The starting place for Septimus' consciousness is generally a point that transcends the object that has occasioned speculation. As a result, he lacks an existential center from which to project his vision of the present into the future. The realization that he is responsible for holding together a vision that threatens momentarily to burst into meaninglessness fills him with terror. "It is I," Septimus confesses in anxiety, "who am blocking the way" (p. 21). The frightening discrepancy between his own experience and the static world toward which his community urges him tempts Septimus to hope that the latter will supply stability. Like Lear in the wilderness, "He would not go mad." Ironically, his attempt to preserve sanity leads him at times to deny the very vision of chaos that distinguishes him from the crowd.

While Clarissa appears bound by the decorum from which Septimus flees, the opening pages of the novel reveal her more affirmative impulses.[9] Virginia Woolf uses the appropriate image of a bird to describe the expansive manner in which Mrs. Dalloway's thoughts take flight from detail. There is, as one of her neighbors describes Clarissa, "a touch of the bird about her" (p. 4). The squeak of hinges and an open door recall the freedom of her youth when the air seemed open. On the London curb she appears "perched," as if in expectation of flight from the confining aspects of practical considerations. While the fact that she must buy flowers for the party motivates her trip to the florist and remains an important concern, she allows the object—flowers—the possibility of opening up a host of other visual connotations. "Things," animated by her presence, are given new life through a complex of intentions far greater than the concern of utility.

Clarissa does not close her eyes once she acknowledges the startling disparity between existential and practical detail; rather she possesses the resiliency to move back and forth between these contrary visions of the world. The booming sounds of Big Ben, the noise of traffic, the prattle of shoppers, through Clarissa's presence are all transformed without loss of their reference in objective time and space. "Heaven only knows why one loves it so," Clarissa speculates while crossing Victoria Street, "how one sees it so, making it up, building it round one, tumbling it, creating it every moment afresh" (p. 5). What she loved, Virginia Woolf assures us, was London on this particular moment of a June morning.

As Clarissa and Septimus stand in separate places on the streets of London, they respond creatively to similar detail: the backfiring of a car, the passing crowds, an airplane skywriting advertisements. Both characters likewise acknowledge an accompanying sense of dread. The unpredictable quality of Being fills the protagonist with a disturbing "solemnity," (the word recurs continually in these opening pages) as if, she first tells us when gazing out the window, "something awful was about to happen" (p. 3). It is the same feeling she acknowledges in that pause before Big Ben strikes, the sense of wonder that we should be at all, that clocks should be striking and that one should be standing there, loving and fearing such phenomena.

Clarissa allows things to reveal themselves in new ways once she has classified them within their familiar context. Her openness to innovation reflects her own independence. She does not require others to supply the meaning of her life. Her critique of "love" and "religion" is essentially an attack upon those who, under the sanction of passion or doctrine, presume to create others in their own image.

Doris Kilman (the name is apt), a Christian convert who serves as tutor to Clarissa's daughter, represents doctrinaire intolerance. Staking her claim in other people, she invades the lonely and mysterious "privacy of the soul" (p. 192). Clarissa finds Miss Kilman difficult because she utilizes others almost exclusively to mirror her own suffering.

People, like things, serve the characters of *Mrs. Dalloway* as means of sustaining their image of themselves. Even the heroine is tempted to make use of others to justify herself. The thought of the tutor's domination of her daughter, arousing Clarissa's feelings to a pitch of hatred, proves a distraction from the recurring sense of emptiness. "Kilman her enemy. That was satisfying; that was real. . . . It was enemies one wanted, not friends" (pp. 265–266). Friends require love, enemies sustain self-love; Clarissa describes her hatred as an expression of the latter. Contrary to her characteristic refusal to label other people or herself—"she would not say of herself, I am this, I am that" (p. 11)—she has created a definitive posture through an act of imposition. Like Peter and Miss Kilman she has chosen a self that relies upon the object of its passion. "Nobody . . . was more dependent upon others" (p. 241), Virginia Woolf suggests through Mrs. Dalloway, than Peter, whose tirades against English society cannot hide his need for recognition.

The objects that fill Clarissa with a *joie de vivre* are largely unnoticed by Peter, who is preoccupied with such general conceptions as "the state of the world . . . Wagner, Pope's poetry, people's characters eternally, and the defects of her own soul" (p. 9). The Hugh Whitbreads and the Lady Brutons of Mrs. Dalloway's world are genuinely lost in the details of writing letters to the *Times* and stocking the royal wine cellar; Peter and Clarissa's old friend Sally Seton oppose such lifeless conformity to outdated traditions with romantic invective. Like Miss Kilman and the psychiatrist Bradshaw,

whose dogma drives Septimus to his death, their aim is to
replace one orthodoxy with another. It is not by chance
that the free and rebellious Sally should choose finally to
marry a wealthy landowner and settle in on the Rosseter estate
while Peter joins the Major Blimps in India.

For Clarissa, marriage like life must supply space
for difference and for license; "a little independence there must
be between people living together day in day out in the same
house" (p. 10), a letting be that with Peter was always impossible. Peter, lacking "the ghost of a notion what anyone
else was feeling" (p. 69), demanded to share everything
and gave nothing out of fear of risking his "point of view."
Clarissa finds such love intolerable.

Richard Dalloway, ignorant of his wife's motives,
bumbling in his effort to communicate his affection to her,
respects, as Peter cannot, the vacant silence that allows relationship: "there is a dignity in people; a solitude; even between
husband and wife a gulf; and that one must respect, thought
Clarissa, watching him [Richard] open the door; for one
would not part with it oneself, or take it, against his will, from
one's husband, without losing one's independence, one's
self respect—" (p. 181). Even Richard, however, causes his
wife unhappiness through misinterpreting her passion to en-
tertain.

Both her husband and former fiancé "laughed at
her very unjustly, for her parties" (p. 183); but this desire to
give parties "for no reason whatever," which Peter felt was
motivated by snobbery and Richard by foolishness expresses
Clarissa's innermost love of Being as well as her inauthenticity;
her parties are "an offering" to life itself. While confessing
that her sense of offering sounds "horribly vague," Virginia
Woolf contrasts the heroine's commitment to others with the
snobbish reserve of Edwardian society. It is the recognition
of and respect for people—"she felt quite continuously a
sense of their existence"—that inspires the heroine to bring
them together. Clarissa's effort to reach "this thing she called

life" (p. 184), leads her to acknowledge that the practical
world cannot sustain her sense of mystery and significance,
that every offering moves relentlessly toward its own annihilation. Clarissa's existential openness leads her continually to
consider non-Being.

Significantly, Septimus' affirmation of life denies
validity to its alternative: the birds in the trees sing to him
that "there is no death" (p. 36). The most terrifying hallucina-
tion his madness must endure is the mirage of the deceased
Evans, "for he could not look upon the dead" (p. 105). This
self-deception enhances Septimus' isolation from others.
Solipsism shelters him from the external evidence that life is
linked with death. Like Sartre's prisoner in "The Wall," he
seeks to sustain the illusion of being immortal in a world
sheltered from human relationships. But his insanity is less
rooted in the eccentric character of his perceptiveness than
in the repression of that meaninglessness which typifies the
times. His madness mirrors the crowd's compulsive pursuit of
self-distraction. Septimus loses himself in a world of romantic
introspection; the Bradshaws, avoiding the abyss of inwardness, seek through science and social hierarchy to bridle those
untoward premonitions that emerge from the depths of
human personality.

Mrs. Dalloway, who cannot bear the subject of
death to be mentioned at her party, is no less a child of her
age. Like the characters in Edward Albee's play named after
Virginia Woolf, the heroine often transposes her anxieties
into merriment, in this case into the poeticism of a line from
Cymbeline. "Fear no more the heat o' the sun," like the sing-
song lyrics "Who's afraid of Virginia Woolf," serve to relieve
the sense of life's absurd conclusion. In so doing, however,
Clarissa experiences the frightening loss of her own personal
being: "Often now this body she wore . . . this body,
with all its capacities, seemed nothing—nothing at all. She had
the oddest sense of being herself invisible; unseen; unknown
. . . this being Mrs. Dalloway; not even Clarissa any more"

(p. 14). As we have seen, such disruptive experiences enrich the heroine's relationship to her world. The sound of Big Ben striking, her Irish cook whistling in the kitchen, or Mr. Dalloway reading the *Times* at breakfast, stand out as "exquisite moments" because they exist tentatively against a backdrop of meaninglessness, against Clarissa's premonition "that it was very, very dangerous to live even one day" (p. 11).

Virginia Woolf explores the manner in which moments of Being come into focus through the awareness of its antithesis at several points in her book.[10] Employing the simile of a fading rocket to convey Rezia's feeling of alienation, she suggests that "the outline of houses and towers" as well as the surrounding countryside, menaced by darkness, exist again "more ponderously" than before: "I am alone; I am alone! she cried, . . . as perhaps at midnight, when all boundaries are lost, the country reverts to its ancient shape, as the Romans saw it, lying cloudy, when they landed, and the hills had no names and rivers wound they knew not where— such was her darkness" (pp. 34–35). Similarly, when Peter Walsh feels threatened by Clarissa's affection, the inanimate objects that fill his hotel room disclose new aspects of significance. "Any number of people had hung up their hats on those pegs. Even the flies, if you thought of it, had settled on other people's noses" (p. 235). More often than not the characters in Virginia Woolf's fictional world retreat before such moments of liberated perspective.

Where Peter and Rezia choose the passive luxury of self-pity, Clarissa, "like a nun withdrawing" from thoughts of life and death, seeks distraction reading memoirs or sewing. In the privacy of an empty room, reading Baron Marbot's description of the retreat from Moscow, Clarissa "could not dispel a virginity preserved through childbirth which clung to her like a sheet." This "emptiness about the heart of life; an attic room" (p. 45), threatens the heroine; it tempts her, as it does Peter, to submerge into oblivion. At other times, in the rising and falling of her needle and thread, she meta-

phorically commits the burden of her consciousness "to some
sea, which sighs collectively for all sorrows, and renews,
begins, collects, lets fall" (p. 59).

Clarissa, however, does not sanctify these with-
drawals. When called back to the world by particular sounds
—the ringing of the door bell while sewing, the sound of
Richard opening a door when reading—she greets such inter-
ruptions with the enthusiasm that characterizes her openness
to life. Lying awake, on her narrow bed, unable to sleep,
she hears below "the click of the handle released as gently
as possible by Richard, who slipped upstairs in his socks and
then, as often as not, dropped his hot-water bottle and swore!
How she laughed!" (p. 47).

From the emptiness of solitude Clarissa gains a
new relationship to external phenomena. The most important
vision that intrudes upon her is that of an old lady she has
often seen through the parlor window. Clarissa's response to
this unknown woman, framed in the window of an adjoining
house like some archetypal inhabitant from a world unrealized,
recalls Virginia Woolf's awe before the presence of Mrs.
Brown. The encounter occurs twice in the course of the novel.

The old lady is first mentioned in contrast to Doris
Kilman. As Clarissa looks across the space that separates the
two buildings, her thoughts pursue Miss Kilman's unwillingness to let others be themselves. As if in benediction, she
blesses the old lady's unfettered movements across the way:
"Let her climb upstairs if she wanted to; let her stop; then
let her, as Clarissa had often seen her, gain her bedroom,
part her curtains, and disappear again into the background"
(p. 191).

The old lady's activity is all the more extraordinary
to Clarissa because it appears to follow the sounds of Big
Ben striking the half hour. Through her movements the finger
of time descended "down, into the midst of ordinary things
. . . making the moment solemn." Like Mrs. Brown's gestures,
which offer few particulars upon which to construct her

history, the neighbor's motions reveal few descriptive facts. In life and art, however, such details are of secondary importance. "Why creeds and prayers and mackintoshes? when, thought Clarissa, that's the miracle, that's the mystery; that old lady" (p. 193).

The ability to see and to wonder at the existence of another human being may appear to be a somewhat obvious virtue. And yet sometime between September 1929 and December 1930, Ludwig Wittgenstein, during his only public lecture at Cambridge, given to the same small group of "Heretics" before which the novelist read her paper on "Mrs. Brown," felt called upon to emphasize for his learned audience the distinction between "the scientific way of looking at a fact," and "the experience of seeing the world as a miracle"; he equates the latter with "wondering at the existence of the world."[11] It is tempting to speculate that Virginia Woolf, who met the philosopher a number of times, might have heard about Wittgenstein's lecture.[12] Regardless of their possible communication, Woolf and Wittgenstein were aware of the complexity involved in their distinction and both felt called upon to make it.

Mrs. Dalloway expresses its author's distaste for the doctrinaire assumptions of an age bent on "solutions." With a fine touch of satire, the novelist describes Bradshaw—a patron of the arts—stopping to scrutinize one of the Dalloways' etchings: "He looked in the corner for the engraver's name" (p. 294). The famous psychiatrist worships, as we have seen, a formidable deity: "Conversion is her name and she feasts on the wills of the weakly, loving to impress, to impose, adoring her own features stamped on the face of the populace" (p. 151). As with Mr. Smith on the train to London, Bradshaw's strength relies upon the weakness of others. The hostess reveals upon seeing him later in the evening: "One wouldn't like Sir William to see one unhappy" (p. 278).

No doctrine of religion or love could hope to solve the "supreme mystery" that grasps Clarissa before the parlor

window. The mystery which Miss Kilman or Peter might
say they had solved, "but Clarissa didn't believe either of them
had the ghost of an idea of solving, was simply this: here
was one room; there another" (p. 193). As Heidegger stressed
in his inaugural lecture, the important consideration about
Being is not "what" or "how" it is, but rather "that" it is, and
that one stands miraculously separated from another by a
nowhere, by a gulf of nothing.[13]

At the time of this first encounter with the old
woman, Mrs. Dalloway is essentially a spectator. Her existential involvement occurs later at the height of her party when
the hostess overhears Dr. Bradshaw talking about the suicide
of a young patient (Septimus). With the intrusion of that
forbidden subject—"Oh! thought Clarissa, in the middle of my
party, here's death" (p. 279)—she withdraws in panic into
a little room which the Prime Minister has just left. The
chamber is empty, with only an impress upon the chairs to
record that moment of history. "Alone in her finery," with
neither guests nor routine to distract her, Mrs. Dalloway's
crisis begins.

Significantly, the heroine's effort to face death
recalls Virginia Woolf's temptation to account for the reality
of Mrs. Brown within a fabric of details. Clarissa first strives
to understand the young man's suicide through a context of
factual description. "He had thrown himself from a window.
Up had flashed the ground; through him, blundering, bruising,
went the rusty spikes. There he lay with a thud, thud, thud
in his brain, and then a suffocation of blackness. So she saw
it." But the details of the tragedy prompt her to consider:
"Why had he done it? And the Bradshaws talked of it at her
party!" There follows an interesting shift as Clarissa apparently reverses the meaning of "it": "She had once thrown a
shilling into the Serpentine, never anything more. But he had
flung it away." Both life and death are bound indistinguishably
in the impersonal pronoun, one as obscure as the other;
what has Septimus lost and to what must Clarissa return?

("She would have to go back; the rooms were still crowded; people kept on coming.") The question of death not only has led the heroine to the question of life but has confused the two, recalling Heidegger's presupposition that Being and non-Being are inseparable. In the midst of this confusion, she establishes a meaning that redeems Septimus' obscure action: "A thing there was that mattered; a thing, wreathed about with chatter, defaced, obscured in her own life, let drop every day in corruption, lies, chatter. This he had preserved. Death was defiance. Death was an attempt to communicate" (p. 280).[14]

Clarissa (echoing the novelist's experience with Mrs. Brown) identifies herself with a human being attempting to preserve the sanctity of his soul from all who seek to control it. In so doing, however, she accepts, as Septimus cannot, the dread of holding the power of life and death in her own hands: "There was the terror; the overwhelming incapacity, one's parents giving it into one's hands, this life, to be lived to the end, to be walked with serenely; there was in the depths of her heart an awful fear" (p. 281).

Heidegger's lecture defines dread as man's anxiety over having nothing to rely on save his own courage to be. In discussing the effects of dread he utilizes a linguistic example that illuminates the passage above as well as Virginia Woolf's persistent use of the indefinite pronoun "one": "In dread we are 'in suspense' (*wir schweben*). Or, to put it more precisely, dread holds us in suspense because it makes what-is-in-totality slip away from us. Hence we too, as existents in the midst of what-is, slip away from ourselves along with it. For this reason it is not 'you' or 'I' that has the uncanny feeling, but 'one.' In the trepidation of this suspense where there is nothing to hold on to, pure *Da-sein* is all that remains."[15]

The sense of Septimus' suicide as somehow "her disaster—her disgrace" leads the heroine to confess that she has led an inauthentic life: "She had wanted success. Lady Bexborough and the rest of it." But through her self-depreca-

tion at having "lost herself in the process of living" come
recollections of moments when the shield has glimmered
and she has perceived, like Wordsworth, a depth in experience.
Walking to the window she is shocked to see the old lady a
second time, now staring straight at her under a sky whose
solemnity is more than romantic orchestration: "She was
going to bed. And the sky. It will be a solemn sky, she had
thought, it will be a dusky sky, turning away its cheek
in beauty. But there it was—ashen pale, raced over quickly by
tapering vast clouds. It was new to her. The wind must have
risen. She was going to bed, in the room opposite. It was
fascinating to watch her, moving about, that old lady, crossing
the room, coming to the window. Could she see her?" (p. 283).

The gulf that separates one room from the other is
now a mysterious and enveloping presence through which
the old lady (who initially gained Clarissa's consciousness as
an alternative to Miss Kilman) appears miraculously free
of all intentions; like the sky she is no object but a presence
that involves Clarissa's joyous response. Septimus' death
has expanded the heroine's world: "The clock began striking.
The young man had killed himself; but she did not pity him;
with the clock striking the hour, one, two, three, she did not
pity him, with all this going on. There! the old lady had put
out her light! the whole house was dark now with this
going on, she repeated, and the words came to her, Fear no
more the heat of the sun. She must go back to them. But what
an extraordinary night! She felt somehow very like him—
the young man who had killed himself" (p. 283). The
extraordinary strangeness of "all this" (her phrase includes
the party behind her and the scene before her) evokes wonder
in Clarissa that requires history, not death, to sustain it. Like
the narrator of Keats's ode, she returns to the "sole self"
through whose artistry alone vision achieves historicity.
Her decision to go back—"she must assemble. She must find
Sally and Peter" (p. 284)—is no reversal. Resisting the temptation to withdraw, Clarissa preserves the gift of her own

presence by reentering the party she has created.[16] While she
remains at the close a perfect hostess, her resolve to share
with her friends the life she has experienced in solitude
marks her existential triumph.

As Clarissa returns to the party, Peter and Sally are
criticizing their friend and hostess in terms that the novelist
herself often employed against society matrons such as
Mrs. Dalloway. Clarissa's world, however, held great appeal
for Virginia Woolf. During the planning and composition
of *Mrs. Dalloway*, her diary reveals a distaste for her heroine
that camouflages a preference for upperclass decorum. The
same entry refers to Joyce's *Ulysses* with snobbish condescension one might expect to hear from Lady Bruton: "the
book of a self taught working man, and we all know how
distressing they are, how egotistic, insistent, raw, striking, and
ultimately nauseating. When one can have the cooked flesh,
why have the raw?"[17]

Lytton Strachey's impression that Virginia Woolf
covered Clarissa very remarkably with her own personality
occasioned no disagreement from the novelist. I suspect
that she was not unaware of her ambivalent feeling toward
Mrs. Dalloway. It is fair to suggest that her indictment of
Peter's and Sally's inability to see Clarissa is a criticism of her
own prejudices. She repeatedly states that her writing was
a struggle for illumination. Recording on May 26, 1924, how
her efforts with *Mrs. Dalloway* have resulted in its "becoming
more analytical and human . . . less lyrical," Virginia Woolf
adds, as if to stress that her aim is phenomenological rather
than impressionistic, that "to see human beings freely
and quickly is an infinite gain to me."[18] Through *Mrs. Dalloway*, she has confronted "the other"; her creation of Clarissa
Dalloway involved an existential act of self-examination.

The values of the age prevent Sally and Peter from
seeing Clarissa. Sally's passion for success leads her to assume
that Clarissa has left the party to cultivate more important
guests. (Peter accounts for her absence on the same grounds.)

Clarissa Dalloway

While Sally's despair of relationship—"she often went into her garden and got from her flowers a peace which men and women never gave her" (pp. 293–294)—characterizes an important theme of the novel, she remains ironically loyal to the predilections of English society. Countering Clarissa Dalloway's social accomplishments with her own less subtle sense of success, she assures all that she has done things too: "I have five sons" (p. 284).

Both friends are quick to condemn as snobbery Clarissa's failure to reach them. They assume that to communicate she must renounce her world for theirs: a world of emotion recollected in tranquillity. Sally, and to a lesser extent Peter, have chosen to live largely in retrospect, preserving autonomy against the unexpected intrusion of foreign ideas and unsettling passions. Significantly, Clarissa responds with affection to those alien qualities in Sally she might well censure: "She [Sally] had the simplest egotism, the most open desire to be thought first always, and Clarissa loved her for being still like that" (p. 261).

Sally's life is over—it is the young who are beautiful, she tells her companion as they watch the Dalloways' youthful daughter. Clarissa, rejuvenated by the presence of an old woman, authenticates the existential faith that man is the future of man; reentering the party she reconstitutes the meaning that defines her life.[19]

While Peter argues with Sally's repudiation of others, Clarissa serves to recall the image of himself he wants to remember: the martyr of objective time and an insensitive society. His supposed independence, his affirmation of privacy as a state in which "one may do as one chooses," masks his own difficulties. As Peter himself admits (echoing Clarissa's earlier observation): "it had been his undoing" (p. 230).

The confusion is part of Peter's makeup. While he replies to Sally that he prefers human beings to cabbages (a phrase that Clarissa recalls when she first thinks about her former fiancé), throughout the novel he asserts a preference for solitude. "Now, at the age of fifty-three," he tells us in Regent Park following his sexual fantasy, "one scarcely needed people any more" (p. 119). The instant of sunshine, like the make-believe escapade with the young woman he has trailed, is enough to sustain his self-centered world. Even Daisy, the woman he intends to marry, exists in his mind as a weapon against Clarissa and as a mirror for indulging his Byronic pose.

Clarissa's message—"Heavenly to see you"—that he finds waiting at his hotel, "was like a nudge in the ribs. Why couldn't she let him be?" (p. 234). Although he asserts that "nothing would induce him to read it again," his romantic self-pity requires the love of a woman that cannot be his. Peter's vow never again to allow a woman to hurt him as Clarissa has is sham. He maintains at great expense the torment that defines and victimizes him. His plea for her to "let him be" is the ironic inversion of Clarissa's respect for the independence of others.

Peter and Sally, however, are no less human by virtue of their inauthenticity. The fear that drives them to dominate others is stamped upon Clarissa's world and no doubt our own. If Peter has denied (more than once) the sanctity of the human heart by reducing Clarissa to "the perfect hostess," on other occasions he has responded to such mystery. Early in the book he describes the magical quality of her parties. Clarissa, he confesses, has "that extraordinary gift, that woman's gift, of making a world of her own wherever she happened to be." During her parties it was not what she did or said that one remembered but rather the extraordinary sense of her being there, "There she was" (pp. 114–115).

In the closing scene, as Clarissa moves from her small room toward Peter, her miraculous presence fills him once again with an undefinable sense of terror and ecstasy; reduced to wonder he can only exclaim: "It is Clarissa." The novel's last words, reiterating Peter's messianic invocation

Clarissa Dalloway

—"For there she was"—challenge each critic's effort to fathom
Mrs. Dalloway. Is the statement a final irony—Peter's romantic
affirmation of a presence that sustains his melancholy—or
does the reader respond with similar apostolic fervor to
Clarissa as being there in some special way?[20] Since Virginia
Woolf sought to portray the mysterious reality of character
it is fitting that, finally, this question remains unanswered.

Rose Wilson

Graham Greene's novel of the thirties pictures an
abysmal environment that relentlessly bullies his heroine's
expectations. Rose's experience of hell, beginning in Snow's
restaurant the moment she is involved with Pinkie, continues
to the end of the novel as she walks toward "the worst horror
of all," the phonograph recording of his loathing for her.
Although Greene plays upon the girl's innocence in a manner
that suggests Gothic melodrama, she ensures a praise for
Brighton Rock beyond the "masterpiece of horror" proclaimed
on paperback editions.[1] Pinkie, the teen-age killer who disrupts Rose's undistinguished career as tearoom waitress, like
the lieutenant of Greene's following novel, *The Power and
the Glory*, prefers "the vast superiority of vacancy" to a world
he has inherited. The heroine, bound to the boy first by
circumstance and then through choice, finds the possibility of
new life while sharing his dark nihilism.

Far removed from the mannered society of *Mrs.
Dalloway*, the inhabitants of Brighton's amusement park
atmosphere reflect the same compulsions Virginia Woolf
described a decade earlier. Like Clarissa, Rose achieves authenticity in relationship to those who deny her the right to exist
apart from their intentions. Garcin's remark at the close
of Jean-Paul Sartre's *No Exit*—"There's no need for red-hot
pokers. Hell is—other people!"—seems strikingly applicable to
the characters of *Brighton Rock*. Pinkie, new in his position
as leader of a small protection racket, must deal with the
consequences of murdering an informer named Fred Hale,
in Brighton on a publicity stunt for a London newspaper.
Hale's job is to pose as the fictitious Kolley Kibber, pictured
on the front page of the *Daily Messenger*, discreetly distribu-
ting Kolley Kibber cards worth money to the finder; the reader
lucky enough to recognize him as the "mystery man" wins
the newspaper's daily prize. His murder, at the outset of the
novel, precipitates the triangular relationship between Pinkie,
Rose, and Ida Arnold, the sensual, fun-loving tart who,
having met Hale in a pub, decides to make those guilty pay for

killing him. Pinkie's public freedom is threatened by Ida and his private life by Rose, the Brighton waitress he must marry to preserve his alibi. In his effort to confuse the police as to the time of Hale's death, Pinkie orders his gang to deposit Kolley Kibber cards after the murder has taken place. Unfortunately, Spicer leaves a card under a tablecloth in the restaurant in which Rose works. Afraid that the waitress might have observed it was Spicer and not Hale who deposited the card, the boy moves to ensure her silence. A wife cannot be made to testify against her husband; ironically, the girl's unconditional love for him requires no such safeguard. Careless of others, incapable of trust, the sadistic young leader is driven by enemy and ally, like Milton's Satan, "deeper than he'd ever meant to go."

Although Pinkie rejects Brighton "culture," echoed along the boardwalk in the lyrics of tranquillizing love songs, his life has been shaped by the power structure of a society based on self-interest. Like Ida, who seeks little men she can "mother" and direct, Pinkie exists by manipulating those less strong than he. While he reacts with "furious distaste" to Ida's "dandy world," where funerals are fun and sex free and natural, it is a familiar and perhaps reassuring sight to him. The crowd's unquestioning allegiance to the world as it is confirms his destructive doctrine. He can comprehend the enemy; Rose's loyalty is beyond his unawakened imagination. Thoughout the novel the boy's critique of Ida is a damning indictment of the bourgeois complacency her actions advocate, yet his perversity requires that such optimistic illusions thrive.

Bound by the traditions of her class, Ida "was prepared to cause any amount of unhappiness to anyone in order to defend the only thing she believed in . . . There was something dangerous and remorseless in her optimism, whether she was laughing in Henneky's or weeping at a funeral or a marriage."[2] Her interest in Rose's future is no less destructive than Pinkie's. Rose, unwilling to be influenced

by facts about the murder, threatens Ida's world as well as
Pinkie's. Her arguments to the girl, based on "experience," all
emphasize that love is unreliable since people are unreliable.
Ida's passion for the predictable has transformed intimacy
into a "peep show" where all the moves are known, where
her boy friend's impotence is comfortably anticipated, and
where disappointment itself is often a luxury.

Other people disturb Ida and Pinkie because they
invite an untracked future, seldom predictable and rarely safe.
Colleoni, ruler of Brighton's underworld, is dangerous, but
not in the same way. When the powerful racketeer orders his
men to "carve" the boy, this unexpected act makes sense
within Pinkie's cynical view of human nature. Similarly, Ida's
"eye for an eye" philosophy, in addition to her theories
on love, exists within the patterned framework of a world she
has conditioned herself to see.

Like *Mrs. Dalloway, Brighton Rock* is more than
incidentally concerned with perception. Pinkie avoids considerations of how others feel or see, while Ida looks upon
everything as a projection of her own wish fulfillment. Drewitt,
the gang's corrupt lawyer, spends his leisurely moments at
the window, searching in quiet desperation for the familiar
objects that sustain his sanity. All seek in prescriptive vision
safeguards against unfamiliar experience.

Fear of the unknown in general and death in
particular determines the manner in which Greene's characters
see the world. Pinkie sublimates his view of life as "dying
slowly" into a ruthless commitment to destructiveness. Ida,
on the other hand, shuns the thought of death: "Nothing could
ever make her believe that one day she too, like Fred, would
be where the worms . . . her mind couldn't take that track;
she could go only a short way before the points automatically
shifted and set her vibrating down the accustomed line"
(p. 192). Even Fred Hale's murder does not alter her vision of
the world. "She saw only the Brighton she knew: she hadn't
seen anything different even the day Fred died" (p. 93). Both

Six Existential Heroes

Ida and Pinkie seek to create a world devoid of fear. Ironically, their efforts lead both to deny life. At the close, as the boy falls over a cliff, acid consuming his flesh, Pinkie is united with the nothingness he has sought: "It was as if he'd been withdrawn suddenly by a hand out of any existence—past or present, whipped away into zero—nothing" (p. 327). Ida, known to the crowd as Lily (the flower of funerals) offers men like Hale a kind of death.

The opening of Greene's novel expresses in parable the theme of man's anxious flight from Being. Hale's quest for anonymity, motivated by the knowledge that "they meant to murder him," has the quality of a modern morality play.[3] He is Everyman. His fears over life and death are the foundation upon which the novel rests. Hale's anticipation of death has separated him from nature and society: "He didn't belong —belong to the early summer sun, the cool Whitsun wind off the sea, the holiday crowd." Faced with this threat, he seeks to lose himself in the crowd. His present vocation fulfills his compulsion to remain anonymous: "From childhood he had loved secrecy, a hiding place, the dark" (p. 18).

The evasions by which he formerly has existed, however, are no longer possible. The summer vacationers who swarm from trains and busses onto the hot Brighton boardwalk cannot save him from the gang's retribution. Death, personified in Pinkie, has cornered Hale in a bar and identified him as Fred. At the same time, Hale seeks the release of death; as Ida perceives during their taxicab ride: "I don't like to see a fellow throw up the sponge that way" (p. 20). The little newsman chooses to withdraw from the realization that he is going to die, first through "the temporary courage of another whisky," then by deluding himself that "he was safe with the fifty thousand visitors," and, finally, in Ida's motherly dispensation, "the confidence of her big body." Ida is like the shadows he sought as a child: his "withered and frightened brain" soon succumbs to the "comfort and peace," to the "touch of the nursery" that she offers. The

mystery of his death—Did his heart stop before the murder?
—only adds to the evidence that he chose to die before the
mob ever reached him. Lacking Pinkie's courage to murder God,
Hale destroys himself.

Like the three characters of *No Exit*, then, Hale,
Ida, and Pinkie express interdependently the limits of their
world. Each exists in macabre counterpoint to the others, in a
hell of his own making. Their circumstance represents a wider
view of the human condition manifest in Drewitt's quote
from Faustus: "Why, this is Hell, nor are we out of it"
(pp. 281–282).

Brighton reveals a holiday of empty men who find
the cool Whitsun wind ineffectual. Like Sartre's characters,
they cannot or will not break through their loneliness and fear
into existential relationship.[4] For Sartre man's estrangement
is final, since God is nonexistent or absent. Greene's God
does not appear to offer man any more tangible assistance.
Only an *ex machina* force could pull mankind from its tragic
inability to love. There is disheartening truth in Ida's reply to
Rose's plea that "people change," that Pinkie may not be
past all hope: "Oh, no, they don't. Look at me. I've never
changed. It's like those sticks of rock: bite it all the way
down, you'll still read Brighton. That's human nature"
(p. 266). The facts suggest Ida is right. Rose's alternative, however, is based on other criteria.

Greene's heroine has left her working-class home to
take a job with two possessions: "an immense store of trivial
memories" (p. 61) and the "expectations" derived from love
songs and movies. A romantic past and future mask an existence replete with abject poverty, crippling disease, and
hopeless ignorance. During her ordeal with Pinkie she learns
to create new meaning from those realities that define her
present. Society offers Rose little help. Deprived of secular
education, schooled in Christian dogma by a church without
passion, subsisting in a ghetto that has reduced her parents
to grotesque shadows of indifference, the heroine's obstacles

seem insurmountable. Since her involvement with the boy
killer occurs on her first day of work, even fortune appears
hostile.

We first see the young waitress interrupting Pinkie's
search for the card Spicer has carelessly placed under the
tablecloth. Her frightened look fills him with scorn: "[She
is] one of those girls who creep about, he thought, as if they
were afraid of their own footsteps." But for the sex he could be
describing Hale. Rose, drawn to the shabby youth by a sense
of their common background, shows a friendliness which
only infuriates him: "He despised her quiet, her pallor, her
desire to please: did she also observe, remember . . .?" (pp.
30–31). He soon discovers that her memory is perfect: she is
fully aware that it was not Fred Hale (the advertised Kolley
Kibber) who left his card at her table.

Rose's permissiveness, distinct from Hale's, reflects
the girl's unconditional concern; she wants to make Pinkie
happy for no apparent reason. When, on their first date, Pinkie
in a fit of sensual rage pinches her wrist until his nails nearly
meet, she tells him, fighting back tears, to continue "if you
like doing that" (p. 65). While repeatedly bending to his
will, Rose preserves the hope for better days that distinguishes
her life from Pinkie's intentions. The boy's unshaken belief
in "flames and damnation" cannot deter her anxious faith that
heaven is no less an eventuality than hell.

Pinkie marries Rose to ensure that her knowledge of
the Kolley Kibber card will not endanger him. Ironically,
her love threatens his freedom in a way he had not foreseen.
Dreaming of the day that he, not Colleoni, "owns" Brighton,
the boy conceives of freedom exclusively in terms of
strength: the power to do anything he pleases. Although
raised in the same neighborhood of Brighton by similarly dis-
interested parents, Rose somehow transcends the values
that have conditioned his solipsism. Her receptiveness discloses
the possibility of relationship. She makes one small demand
upon her husband: that he recognize her love for him. Her

expectation, however, challenges his wish to be free of all
human contacts, of "other people's emotions washing at
the brain" (p. 311). Pinkie realizes the girl's silent threat;
"He could feel her all the time trying to get at him" (p. 230).
At the climax of the novel, when he is pressing her to suicide,
Greene describes a similar pressure in apparently theological
terms: "An enormous emotion beat on him; it was like
something trying to get in; the pressure of gigantic wings
against the glass" (p. 322). Like the crowds of vacationers,
impervious to the Whitsun spirit (symbolized by the wind and
rain), Pinkie denies entrance to Grace capable of transforming his hatred into love.

    At other times the young killer acknowledges an
alternate freedom that he appears powerless to receive. A few
hours after his wedding, music in a movie brings anxiety:
"He felt constriction and saw—hopelessly out of reach—a
limitless freedom: no fear, no hatred, no envy" (p. 239). Then,
when forced to give up his chastity, he feels momentarily
liberated "by the strangeness of his experience." Although
he soon incorporates the sexual act into his own familiar
vision of damnation, for a time the passion he feels for his new
wife humanizes him: "He had exposed himself and nobody
had laughed . . . A faint feeling of tenderness woke for his
partner in the act. He put out a hand and pinched the lobe of
her ear" (p. 243). In relaxing his will to control, Pinkie falls
prey to the unconscious fear of rejection he so long has
repressed. Later that night, haunted by images from the past,
he awakens, burdened with the same "appalling emptiness"
he had felt when challenged earlier by Rose's love. The sense
of alienation drives him outside, where he experiences the
night world in a way that for him is unique: "He could see
basement railings, a cat moving, and, reflected on the dark sky,
the phosphorescent glow of the sea." Each detail reveals
itself in the darkness as if for the first time. "It was a strange
world: he had never been alone in it before. He had a
deceptive sense of freedom as he walked softly down towards

the channel" (p. 251). On a road outside Brighton, feeling
the lightness of the country air, Pinkie even imagines he has
escaped his former world. The moment of introspection,
however, is brief; recapturing his senses, he vows an end to
such obscurely dangerous interludes. The fact that Rose
knows what he has done demands logic: "He had won a move
and lost a move: they couldn't *make* her give evidence, but
she knew" (p. 250). Like Nietzsche's ugliest man, he cannot
abide a witness to his inwardness. Moreover, Rose's affection,
in the face of his evil, offends reason. Rejecting life, he concludes with ruthless finality that "only death could ever
set him free."

While Pinkie lives outside the law, the vocation he
has inherited from Kite, the gang's former leader, supplies
him a place in Brighton. He confesses to his loyal henchman
Dallow: "I'd feel a stranger away from here" (p. 295).
Similarly, Ida dismisses the unfamiliar from her life: "She
had no pity for something she didn't understand." The word
"stranger," like "death," Greene tells us, means nothing to
her: "There was no place in the world where she felt a
stranger" (p. 94).

Rose is receptive to new experience as Pinkie and
Ida are not. Awakening the morning after her wedding, she is
not startled to find her husband gone. Rose expects to be
surprised by "this foreign world"—she was, after all,
"a stranger in the country of mortal sin." Since Pinkie has
left her with no duties, it is primarily the absence of routine
with which she must deal. No alarm signals the time to arise;
instead, her sleep is interrupted by the morning sunlight pouring through a curtainless window. When she hears a clock
somewhere in the building striking eleven, acknowledging
that "all her life she had lived in hearing the same one till
now," she responds with joy to the new sounds. For perhaps the first time she feels proudly free to do anything
that pleases her.

Although enraptured by such "immense freedom,"

Rose Wilson

Rose, like Clarissa Dalloway, does not forget those social
rituals that have always defined her relationship to others.
"She lay there wondering what a wife had to do" (p. 253).
The kitchen, on the floor below her bedroom, merely increases
the atmosphere of absence that Greene has already emphasized: "On the window-sill there were two empty sardine tins;
a dirty saucer lay under the table for a cat which wasn't there;
a cupboard stood open full of empties . . . somebody a long
time ago had set a mousetrap by a hole but the bait had been
stolen and the trap had snapped on nothing at all." When
Dallow finally stumbles sleepily into the room, he informs
Rose that no tasks exist here: "This is Liberty Hall" (pp.
255–256).

Like Pinkie the night before, Rose feels compelled
to take a walk. Whereas the darkness paradoxically revealed
an objective world to the boy, "in the early sun" Rose discovers her freedom from the external world. As she
watches the crowd of Brighton inhabitants shuffling back
and forth on accustomed tracks—"People coming back from
seven-thirty Mass, people on the way to eight-thirty Matins"
—the Sunday church bells no longer bind her to the passion-
less routine of her former religious life. In spite of her new
sense of abandon, however, she respects, as Pinkie cannot, the
world she has rejected. The others have chosen one way
of life, she has chosen another: "They had their salvation and
she had Pinkie and damnation" (p. 260).

Arriving at Snow's, Rose stands outside the
restaurant to observe the familiar routine of setting the tables
for breakfast. On the verge of announcing her freedom from
such drudgery—"She was married. She was a woman. She
was happy"—the bony and immature features of a young
waitress named Maisie suddenly haunt Rose with an image
of her former self. Out of pity for the girl she destroys all
appearance of pleasure and cuts her visit short. Returning home
she finds an unexpected guest whose concern for her happiness is motivated by less enviable passions.

47

Six Existential Heroes

This is not Rose's first meeting with Ida Arnold. Earlier, the woman, informing Rose of Pinkie's crimes, had charged that he did not love her. The girl's reply—"I don't care . . . I love him."—struck the worldly Ida as romantic: "I was like you once. You'll grow out of it. All you need is a bit of experience" (p. 163). Now Ida encounters her with the expectation that experience has had an effect. Her "merciless compassion" contrasts with the pity Rose has just shown the waitress at Snow's. When she discloses her latest evidence, that Pinkie is a murderer, Rose's answer—"Do you think I don't know *that*?" (p. 264)—disarms her. As Ida, at the end of her patience, charges the girl with disregarding right and wrong, Greene once more emphasizes his heroine's strange sophistication: "The woman could tell her nothing she didn't know about these—she knew by tests as clear as mathematics that Pinkie was evil—what did it matter in that case whether he was right or wrong?" (pp. 267–268).

Rose's existential confrontation with Pinkie's evil reveals the same openness that characterizes her dialogues with Ida. A note she had scribbled to her husband, promising "Wherever you go, I'll go too," inspires him to get rid of her through a double suicide pact. Accepting the argument that they cannot escape the police, Rose agrees to kill herself. The decision to commit this last sacrilege, however, does not ignore reality: "If this was the darkest nightmare of all," she reflects in Pinkie's car, "if he didn't love her, as the woman said . . . the wet windy air flapped her face through the rent. It didn't matter: she loved him" (p. 304). Rose, mirroring Christ's love, is willing to die for Pinkie, if not with him.

As they drive through the suburbs of Brighton, the rows of empty villas reveal the "pipedream architecture" of a world that has lost interest in the future. The streets, branching toward the cliffs adjoining the sea, end in the same obscure emptiness, "like the last effort of despairing pioneers to break new country. The country had broken them" (pp. 306–307).

Rose Wilson

They stop first at a hotel to have a drink. The building's Victorian decor, an absurd confusion of time and space, reflects and sustains the anarchy into which Rose has plunged with "terrified patience." A "moorish-Tudor-God-knows-what-of-a-lamp" throws its light over an empty lounge filled with "tombstone" sculptures. "Somebody had broken the hands off one of the statuettes—or perhaps it was made like that, something classical in white drapery, a symbol of victory or despair" (p. 308). Around the tables, stained glass windows display medieval ships, while on the panelled walls rose and lily are joined in the color of gold. Greene describes the waiter as being oddly like and yet different from Pinkie. As in "Liberty Hall," any and all meaning is permitted. Gripped by a sense of "awful unreality," the couple feels compelled "to make conversation."

Emptiness threatens Pinkie as long as he does not fill time with his demoniac intentions. Luckily, the attendant is a former classmate he often had bullied at school—"I used to give him Hell in the breaks"—and so he finds momentary distraction in recalled hatred. When the waiter leaves, the sound of rain on the windows returns to disturb him. Longing for forgetfulness Pinkie seeks to purge his mind of every reminder that strange realities exist outside his understanding. A concealed radio predicting the weather with dispassionate precision seems the only conception of the future he can admit.

Rose's new freedom abruptly ended with Pinkie's suggested suicide. As they leave the hotel, however, the idea grasps her that she is as free to deny his demands as she had been to love him. "It came like a revelation, as if someone had whispered to her that she was someone, a separate creature—not just one flesh with him. She could always escape —if he didn't change his mind . . . Nothing was decided— there was always hope" (p. 321). Waiting in the car for Pinkie to come in out of the rain, "she wanted to tell him that he mustn't stand there, getting wet, because she'd changed her mind." Her unwillingness to define herself apart from others

Six Existential Heroes

once again hinders self-interest.

Greene presents his heroine's decision to follow the boy in Christ-like terms: "She felt responsibility move in her breasts; she wouldn't let him go into that darkness alone" (p. 307). The contrast with Ida's "religious" fervor is striking. Rose is motivated by *caritas*; Ida's dedication to "right" is thoroughly self-indulgent. Her tears at Hale's funeral are a mockery of Jesus: "And Ida wept" (p. 44).

When they reach the vacant lot Pinkie has chosen for the double suicide, the high promontory, full of wet thorn bushes, remind him of Christ's passion; the words of the Mass come back to the boy: "He was in the world . . . and the world knew Him not" (p. 323). But it is his own rejection that recalls Calvary. Instructing Rose with cool and deadly precision in the art of self-destruction, he places the loaded revolver in her hands. With the possibilities for hope all but expended, the frightened heroine momentarily weakens. "Priestly tones remembered from old sermons" offer moral axioms as alternatives to existential commitment; "You can plead for him at the throne of Grace" tempts the girl to recant. Her Christian past urges Rose to renounce a love that requires crucifixion. Aware, however, that it was not duty that distracted her so much as fear of death, she does not allow self-deception to buttress her passion to survive. "If it was a guardian angel speaking to her now, he spoke like a devil—he tempted her to virtue like a sin."

The demand upon Kierkegaard's Abraham "to murder" Isaac challenges him to do God's work by denying the Lord's commandments. Greene treats his heroine's teleological suspension of the ethical as a no less courageous affirmation of faith: "The evil act was the honest act, the bold and the faithful . . . it was a poor love that was afraid to die" (p. 325). Having broken every sacrament, Rose becomes *Brighton Rock*'s existential advocate for a churchless Christianity.[5] Significantly, Greene treats her decision to deny ecclesiastical law as a vehicle for Grace. A voice in the wilderness, unseen like that of the radio announcer, is the gospel (good news) which redeems Rose from the deadly plan. Hearing Pinkie's name shouted through the rain, she puts down the revolver. The timely appearance of the unangelic Ida and Dallow, accompanied by an officer of the no less tarnished Brighton police force, halts the intended suicide. It is, however, Rose's capacity to receive the unexpected as an occasion for hope that establishes the validity of this event. "It seemed to her that this must be news, that this must make a difference. She couldn't kill herself when this might mean good news. It was as if somewhere in the darkness the will which had governed her hand relaxed" (p. 325). Her passion for life distinguishes the heroine in a society whose death wish Greene has described at length. Rose's affirmation of hope in the face of Pinkie's unbending denial strikes the novelist as a greater miracle than her fortuitous rescue. Greene hints at Rose's sanctification as she looks out from the "stained glass" of the old car on a boy stripped of all defenses; through her eyes Pinkie is not the spirit of incarnate evil. Closed to the possibility of a future, his baptism into the world is a ritual of annihilation. As he races toward the cliff, blinded by the vitriol, he seems to shrink "into a schoolboy flying in panic and pain, scrambling over a fence, running on." By contrast, Rose's steadfast presence emerges as phenomenon. The irony of Ida's part in the rescue is compounded when she returns to Henneky's bar to announce the secret of her success: " 'It shows,' Ida Arnold said, 'you only have to hold on' " (p. 327). Thinking solely of herself, she has seen nothing of the girl's virtue.

Why, then, if Rose has endured, does Greene end his book so ambiguously? Must she be placed once again "on the rack of this cruel world?" The answer borders on tautology: She must suffer because she remains in the world.[6] Sean O'Faolain's description of Greene's cosmos applies to Rose: "I suffer, therefore I am."[7] While the revelation the phonograph record holds for the girl is, in fact, a horror greater than anything that has preceded it, we should not presume that this last test will destroy one who has not shunned unexpected facts before.

In adapting *Brighton Rock* to the screen, Terence Rattigan drastically revised the ending.[8] Early in the film Rose drops the unbreakable plastic recording with the words she has never heard: "You may think I love you, but to me you are just an ugly brat and I hate you." At the close of the motion picture she goes with a nun to hear Pinkie's voice saying: "You may think I love you I love you I love you. . . ." The cracked record has apparently saved the day, or at least postponed the crisis.[9] The melodrama comes to the aid of Rose, rejecting the absurd proposition that she can withstand even such "proof" as this.

In the novel's last episode, Greene approaches heresy in affirming Rose's courageous self-reliance. The girl's absurd love for Pinkie survives despite all the evidence pagan and Christian society muster against him. Her faith inspires even the priest, who from the confessional hints at her sainthood. Rose, however, has not sought to escape the demonic. She is not a saint, at least not in Murray Krieger's sense of the word.[10] Reasserting her love for Pinkie, she defies the old man's sense of morality just as she had challenged Ida's notion of right and wrong. Unable to combat such conviction with logic, the priest is led to comment on "the appalling . . . strangeness of the mercy of God." His final instruction to Rose is pointedly ironic: " 'But we must hope,' he said mechanically, 'hope and pray.' 'I want to hope,' she said, 'but I don't know how.' " The priest's doctrine is correct: *Corruptio optimi est pessima.* Rose does not have to know how to hope. Her life is a testimony to that passion.[11] She looks beyond the present before the record has been heard.

> "And if there's a baby . . ."
> He said: "With your simplicity and his force . . .
> Make him a saint—to pray for his father."

> A sudden feeling of immense gratitude broke
> through the pain—it was as if she had been given the
> sight a long way off of life going on again. He said:
> "Pray for me, my child."
> She said: "Yes, oh, yes" (p. 332).

Her last words grasp the possibility that from all this darkness
a new life can emerge. The fact that Rose's love for Pinkie
is not reciprocated must not affect our response. "Even if the
man to whom I say *Thou* is not aware of it in the midst of
his experience," suggests Martin Buber, "yet relation may
exist. For *Thou* is more than *It* realizes."[12] Rose, like Pinkie,
is conscious that existence is a sickness unto death, but her
life extends, as the boy's cannot, absurdly beyond the limits of
this knowledge. Such faith, as Kierkegaard understood,
lives with denial.

THREE / ISAAC McCASLIN

Jean-Paul Sartre compares William Faulkner's historical sense in *The Sound and the Fury*, chronicle of the Compsons, a fictional Southern family, to that of a passenger who sees events through the rear window of a moving automobile: "At every moment, formless shadows, flickerings, faint tremblings and patches of light rise up on either side of him, and only afterwards, when he has a little perspective, do they become trees and men and cars."[1] Such a reduction of experience to hindsight results, he continues, in an atmosphere of suspended time *(l'enfoncement)*. While praising Faulkner's portrayal of inauthenticity[2] Sartre regrets the absence of those characters who might establish a meaningful future on the basis of their own past and present. Quentin Compson's soliloquy, comprising the second section of the novel, reveals a man who, prior to his suicide, has already chosen not to be.

Although Faulkner questioned the point, the impression has remained among many critics that his protagonists prior to 1940 generally withdraw from a noisy and chaotic universe. If meaning exists for the novelist it apparently lies outside the endless and circular repetition of history in an eternity untainted by Being or time. The appearance of Isaac McCaslin in a short story one year after the first publication of Sartre's essay signals the change that is to mark Faulkner's subsequent heroes. Whether or not Faulkner read or heard about Sartre's praise and criticism of his work in 1939 is a matter for conjecture. What seems clear is that Faulkner's subsequent work, and more particularly *Go Down, Moses*, answers the French existentialist's chief objection.

Isaac McCaslin's life is the subject of three important sections of *Go Down, Moses*: "The Old People," "The Bear," and "Delta Autumn." While the first two sections appeared initially as short stories (in somewhat different form), Faulkner intended that they be read as a whole with his hero's education at the center of the narrative.[3]

Six Existential Heroes

"The Old People" describes Isaac's experience at the age of twelve of killing his first deer, and his initiation, through Sam Fathers, son of a Chickasaw Indian chief and a Negro mother, into the sacred ritual of the hunt. "The Bear," made up of five parts, is set four years later, when the boy joins the older men in hunting the indomitable bear, Old Ben. The chapter covers, both chronologically and psychologically, the largest portion of the hero's development. In the midst of this tale occurs a lengthy dialogue between Isaac and his older cousin "Cas" Edmonds, who has raised him. The time is five years after Isaac has witnessed the death of Old Ben, presumably close to the day that he reached his twenty-first birthday. This difficult narrative-within-a-narrative reveals that at the age of sixteen, the boy also deciphered some curious entries he had often read in the large family ledgers about a Negro slave who for some unstated reason drowned herself. At the time he realized that this slave girl had given birth to his grandfather's daughter and twenty-two years later had committed suicide when the same Carothers McCaslin had a son by his half black daughter. In "Delta Autumn" Isaac, now "Uncle Ike," close to eighty, appears on what apparently will be his last trip into the wilderness, encountering two black descendants, a mother and child, of his grandfather McCaslin.

As we shall see, Faulkner's treatment of these events reveals a fundamentally Biblical view of Southern history. It is not just that the spirit of the Old Testament illuminates *Go Down, Moses*. The book's structure as well as the redemptive quality of characters like Isaac McCaslin seems at times to emerge from those religious sources which stirred the novelist's imagination. Faulkner confesses that the writing of his novels and the inspiration from Scripture were often "simultaneous."[4] Most important is the fact that Faulkner's preference for the flesh-and-blood world of the Old Testament helps delineate an existential quality in his new hero.

Isaac McCaslin

William Barrett's summary in *Irrational Man* of the
similarities between Hebraism and Existentialism is particularly useful here. The Biblical figure, Barrett submits, is a
man of faith existing in the concreteness of his own historical
situation. Unlike his Greek counterpart, who stresses the
ideal of theoretical detachment, he is passionately committed
to his own being, his own family tribe and his own God.
In further distinction from the Hellenist, sin prevents him
from identifying the good with the beautiful. Finally,
this Hebraic protagonist's sense of God and eternity is shadowy
and mysterious, suggesting that depth we spoke of earlier
which neither language nor intuition can fathom.[5] As we
shall see, each of these qualities distinguishes the authenticity
Faulkner ascribes to Isaac McCaslin.

In *Go Down, Moses* the Old Testament appears
chiefly through Psalm 22, "My God, my God, why hast thou
forsaken me?" and chapters 19–25 of the Book of Exodus.
Psalm 22 inspires the structure and symbolism in the hunt of
Old Ben; Exodus discloses the context of this central incident.
Although this influence will be developed later, it may
initially prove helpful to list four of the more obvious themes
from Exodus that Faulkner employs. First and most apparent
is Moses and the Israelites camping in the wilderness;
second, the sound of the horn through which God's voice
emerges; third, the gold and silver trinkets the Israelites
take as their legacy from Egypt, and from which they build
their golden calf; and finally Moses sprinkling the blood of
the sacrificed oxen on the people as a sign of God's covenant
and as a sign of election.

Isaac's existential education begins with a Biblical
invocation in the wilderness of Mississippi's Delta country:
"At first there was nothing." From this empty silence emerge
"the voices of the hounds." Almost simultaneously, Sam
Fathers touches him on the shoulder to signal the approaching
buck. The anticipation of what is to occupy the void fills
the boy with fear—"he began to shake, not with any cold"—

not so much in expectation of the kill as in wonder for what is to be seen. "Then the buck was there. He did not come into sight; he was just there."[6] The deer's appearance remains ambiguous. Isaac apparently sees the creature as a result of trembling before an abyss at the heart of nature.

On the level of a hunting story, Faulkner's descriptions are true to the incident described. He develops his Scriptural intention throughout the following two sections. Isaac's perception of the buck, clearly a revelation into the mystery of Being and of creation, recalls the opening verses of the Bible and God's pronouncement: "Let there be light." The stag of the novel does not look like a ghost but rather like the center of all illumination: "as if all of light were condensed in him and he were the source of it, not only moving in it but disseminating it." The image vanishes in the instant it is seen, leaping with its grand antlers into the uncharted "Big Bottom" from which it came. Faulkner soon emphasizes the mythic quality of these creatures' horns.

At the proper instant, Sam instructs the boy to shoot, but, as the narrator immediately indicates: "the boy did not remember that shot at all. He would live to be eighty . . . but he would never hear that shot nor remember even the shock of the gun-butt." What he does recall is Sam's instruction to take hold of its horns, the old Indian hunter bending down in sacramental pose after the deer's throat had been cut, dipping his hands into the "hot smoking blood" (p. 164) and wiping them across the boy's face, and finally, Sam's horn ringing three times in the wet and gray woods bringing the wave of dogs and other men to the scene.

Many philosophers of existence consider the history of Western metaphysics vitiated by what Heidegger has called an incurious "forgetfulness of being" (*Seinsvergessenheit*).[7] The failure to wonder why anything should exist at all, in other words, taking for granted the existence and history of all phenomena as something given, is both an act of self-effacement and a renunciation of man's potentially

creative relationship with other beings. Faulkner's emphasis
upon memory in the education of Isaac McCaslin acknowledges
man's temptation to shrink from the sources and distortions
of that meaning in which he participates. Throughout "The
Bear" and the hunting experience transcribed in "The Old
People" something of importance is revealed to the boy.
In "Delta Autumn" Uncle Ike's effort to transcend his derived,
social prejudices and reaffirm the central event of his life is
no easy task. Ike must preserve an experience that his society
as well as his own temperament apparently denies.[8]

The opening of "The Old People" inquires into the
phenomenology of sense perception. In effect, Faulkner
asks through Isaac's experience, how does the hunter fix the
deer in time and space? What is required in order to make it a
portion of the hunter's own experience? Sartre, we remember, suggested that hell is other people because man instinctively appropriates the other into his frame of vision. Since
Sartre has denied God, that tension definitive of the human condition remains absolute. This appears to be Faulkner's
chief point of criticism directed against Sartre's fiction.[9]
Faulkner's faith in Being is clearly a sense of significance that
passes understanding, rational and intuitive alike. Nature
offers his protagonists few proofs.

When the deer reveals its glory to Isaac, the young
hunter passively submits to the vision. To establish this
experience in time he must, as it were, stake his claim of presence in the passing apparition; he must halt its flight. The act
of shooting the buck represents that symbolic act of
conscious recognition that follows receptiveness. In focusing
his senses upon the deer, formulating a picture in his own
mind, he has made the reality of the other his own experience.[10]
It is not the shooting of the buck that grasps Isaac throughout
his life, however, but the prophetic demand to preserve the
recollection of that phenomenological encounter. Those
like Doris Kilman (Elizabeth's tutor in *Mrs. Dalloway*) who
stake a claim in Being deny expansiveness to life. Isaac's

task in *Go Down, Moses,* as well as in the Scriptures, is to witness and proclaim the unfolding of depth.

While the opening of "The Old People" parallels God's creation, "The Bear" represents man's opportunity to "begin" the life God had intended for him. The opening pages disclose the hunters gathering together in humble expectation of the annual encounter with Old Ben. Their taking of the brown whiskey, like the sacrament of the Eucharist, symbolizes an act of participation, not in the blood they have spilled, but in "the wild immortal spirit" with whom they seek communion. They drink with no expectation of gaining control over virtue and knowledge ("the pagan's base and baseless hope") but rather "in salute" (p. 192) to the revelation they are privileged to experience.

Like the deer who instinctively run in circular patterns, the characters of Faulkner's fictional world move predictably within circles of finite time. But Faulkner implies that there are other worlds, indeed other aspects of Being, whose meaning is constituted by other centers. In the former our beginning, like our ending, is preordained; in the latter we discover the demand to be ourselves. While the decision "to begin" is grounded for the existentialist in the charted, social world, direction is not predetermined by the latter. Counter to the positivist's credo, man is justified in establishing his own direction, which is to say his own starting point, from the diversity of experience at hand. As for the source of that demand "to begin," it remains, as the Hebrew prophet understood, mysterious.

Clarissa Dalloway and Rose Wilson both acknowledge the bondage of time. Rose, we recall, cannot escape the horror of the next "fact" concerning Pinkie's infidelity and Clarissa must return to the party that will once more tempt her to participate in the banalities of Edwardian society. The transcendence each character achieves is rather a new awareness that reshapes their relationship to events. Their lives, or more accurately their histories, commence at the

point when they are capable of affirming the acts in their own
lives that make both their past and future meaningful: in
the case of Rose her loyalty to Pinkie, in Clarissa's life her
less dramatic response before the old lady.

Certain events in our lives grasp us as significant
because for an often undefinable reason we are receptive to the
event and may even have anticipated it. Such happenings,
furthermore, have a somewhat more obvious effect on what
follows. For the Christian, Advent is the normative event
of history, shaping all that precedes and follows. For the Jew,
Moses' revelation on Mount Sinai expresses a similar sense
of centrality.[11] As I have suggested, the experience that Isaac
McCaslin affirms as definitive bears a close resemblance to
the spirit of the latter.

Sam Fathers teaches Isaac how to live in the
wilderness; no less important, he teaches him how to translate
the acts that define this new life into the future. Even Sam's
stories of the past become part of the boy's present. Listening
to him speak, Isaac senses that some of his stories "had not
happened yet but would occur tomorrow . . . that he himself
had not come into existence yet" (p. 171). Terming the old
man's voice "the mouthpiece of the host," Faulkner establishes
him as the prophet of time and of Being. Through the old
man, Isaac learns to face the past iniquity of his family history
as well as the future. But first, like Old Ben, who "had
earned for himself a name, a definite designation like a living
man," Isaac must "earn for himself from the wilderness
the name and state of hunter" (pp. 192–193). To be something,
he must learn to face nothing.

Old Ben, an incarnation of that "dimensionless"
wilderness from which, like the buck, he emerges, symbolizes
the quality of Being which Heidegger suggests is the condition for the emergence and recognition or naming of anything.
The shaggy and tremendous shape, big rather than malev-
olent, elicits dread and abhorrence because it cannot be
"encompassed"; it is "too big for the very country which

was its constricting scope." Like uncharted land, the bear
extends beyond the limits of a fanatically prescriptive society.
Faulkner establishes this sense of the creature's being, prior
to all human formulation, as an element within human
nature itself. The boy confesses that the bear ran in his knowledge and loomed in his dreams "before he ever saw it." But
whereas Isaac and Sam Fathers set out to encounter the bear,
man has generally sought to control and destroy that which
defies his rationalizations: "the little puny humans swarmed
and hacked at [this apotheosis of the old wild life] in a
fury of abhorrence and fear like pygmies about the ankles
of a drowsing elephant" (p. 193). Faulkner's sense of authentic
life is juxtaposed continually with the picture of these "nameless" men invading the wilderness with ax, rail, and plow.
Western civilization labors, for him, as for Heidegger, under
a self-inflicted bondage motivated, according to the novelist, by
greed and cowardice.

  The bear's existence becomes less and less possible
as man fills the wilderness with projections of his own order.[12]
With Old Ben's demise, Sam Fathers dies; he too has no
more space in which to breathe. Like the beast he has hunted
—"Old Priam reft of his old wife and outlived all his sons"
(p. 194)—Uncle Ike becomes the last existing hope in
Faulkner's fictional world for maintaining the recollection
of that Being he has been privileged to know.

  Old Ben, personifying the Big Bottom country in
which they hunt, offers those who search for him a means of
transcending the disparate and conflicting elements in society.
Through this symbol, Faulkner treats the uncontrolled,
unoccupied space in which it is possible for separate beings
to communicate with one another. In the forest, differences of
race and social station are suspended and relationship is
possible. And yet the reader seldom feels impelled to interpret
this interlude as a midsummer night's dream, occasioned
by the enchantment of strange deities. The hunters' vocation
sets their relationship within a well-defined tradition. The

reality of death pervades their existence in the wilderness as
thoroughly as it does in the town. But, while the traditions
of "civilized" Southern society have their roots largely in a
cultivated European tradition, the ritual of the hunt looks
back to the earliest primitive sources of civilization. The
hunters' archetypal encounter with the otherness of the beast
reenacts man's initial encounter, through love, dread, and
death, with his surrounding world. Significantly, primitive
tribes honored and often worshipped their kill believing that
in consuming wild flesh, new sources of life and of Being
were opened to them. As in the work of Virginia Woolf,
Faulkner's effort to trace Western history to its "bottom"
resembles the efforts of philosophers like Husserl and
Heidegger to seek our historical starting point.

 While the Big Bottom offers Faulkner's characters
an openness in which the other can come into view, the
ritual of the hunt also establishes the tragic rhythm through
which man is led to dominate and destroy each redemptive
vision. The event of Isaac's first buck documents the fatality
that accompanies every historical formulation. It is not by
chance that Sam's father, Ikkemotubbe, had named himself
Doom. Paradoxically, then, "the beginning" that Sam Fathers
fosters in Isaac is related to "the ending." In Faulkner,
Being and nothingness are juxtaposed as closely as Being
and time. In this sense, the pursuit of Old Ben, once translated from the expectancy of dreams into the reality of the
hunt, confronts Isaac with the limits of life. The inevitable end
of something begun motivates man's efforts to deny his own
existence.

 When Sam suggests that someday a hunter will kill
Old Ben and Isaac replies that it must be on the last day,
"when even he don't want it to last any longer" (p. 212), Isaac
has not yet lost the illusion that the bear is eternal; he has
not faced the reality that every beginning has validity because
it participates in its own ending. The final lesson he learns
before becoming a man is that death, personified in Lion,

the wild dog which Sam tames to hunt the bear, is the inevitable condition for life.

Lion, "an animal almost the color of a gun or pistol barrel" (p. 216), is the necessary weapon that brings success to the hunters' many years of effort. The dog's devouring destructiveness, however, is "a cold and almost impersonal malignance like some natural force" (p. 218). Isaac, watching Lion and the dog's human counterpart, Boon Hogganbeck, finds that nature must be controlled if human history is to survive.

The realization that Sam Fathers was the "chief" within a hierarchy of descending order through Boon to Lion, is more than Faulkner's affirmation of the structures he has derived from his Southern environment. Although "Sam's hand touched Lion first" he is not allowed to own him, much less question the wishes of a white man. While Isaac does not oppose the white man's domination of the black, he sees and affirms that Sam's kingship is of a deeper order. When Isaac perceives that Sam's heroism stands within the very society that denies him equal opportunity, in spite of inequity, "then," Faulkner tells us, "he became a man" (p. 222).

The white man's domination of the black describes the former's relationship to nature. This compulsion appears in his rape of the land and in his efforts to order the wilderness. Once Isaac has mapped the forest with such precision, he has intruded upon its inviolable Being as surely as his first bullet had entered the buck. In his fifteenth year even the mysterious place in which he had first been grasped by the presence of the bear is now a spot from which he can judge exactly where the dogs had jumped Old Ben. As a man, however, Isaac can endure this end as he has faced the beginning. He neither hates nor fears Lion because he has begun to accept the inevitable end of each beginning: "It seemed to him that there was a fatality in it. It seemed to him that something, he didn't know what, was beginning; had already begun. It was like the last act on a set stage. It was

the beginning of the end of something, he didn't know what
except that he would not grieve." His participation in Being,
although tainted as it must be by the knowledge of human
depravity, is a source of joy. "He would be humble and
proud that he had been found worthy to be a part of it too
or even just to see it too" (p. 226).

Isaac dimly understands the sad necessity of Lion;
the identification Faulkner draws between the wild dog and
Boon, however, suggests a less obvious curse under which
man labors. Boon, whose life is one with the conventions
that define his society, is finally incapable of achieving freedom in the forest, as the closing pages of "The Bear" indicate.
Whether hunting bear or chipmunk, his being, like that of
Isaac's ancestors who have revelled in the ownership of
land, expresses the passion to appropriate the life he pursues.
Flinging himself "astride the bear . . . his legs locked around
the bear's belly," Boon plunges his weapon in a deadly
rhythm of annihilation. Isaac, watching "the glint of the
knife as it rose and fell" (p. 241), both man and dog careless
of Old Ben's "presence," senses the rape that is taking place.

Sam realizes the qualities in Lion that have made
him "the dog" to trap Ben: "He don't care. He don't care
about nothing or nobody" (p. 220). His name, the recurring
Biblical title of the Satanic enemy, "walking up and down"
the earth (Job 1:7) "seeking whom he may devour"
(1 Peter 5:8) mirrors Faulkner's sense of the demonic in
human history.

Whether by intention or not, Faulkner's treatment of
the hunters, closing in, with Lion and the other dogs, on a
creature whose features join elements of pagan sovereignty
(King Priam) and Christ's suffering (the bear's pierced
paw) echoes first the Psalmist then Jesus himself crying out
for a God who has forsaken him. Having witnessed the death
of Old Ben through the inevitable intervention of Lion and
Boon, Isaac, in the long dialogue with his cousin, is driven to
consider if God is indeed just or for that matter relevant.

Implicit in Psalm 22 is the poet's dual sense of God's reality and of God's absence. The plea to deliver his life "from the power of the dog," from the enemies who gape upon him with their mouths, like "a ravening and a roaring lion," apparently influenced Faulkner's formulation of "The Bear."

At age sixteen, Isaac has experienced the death of Old Ben and realized the tragic exploitation of black people by the McCaslin family. The entry in the old family ledger, long enigmatic, now reveals itself. First the formal facts: "Eunice Bought by Father in New Orleans 1807 $650 dolars. Marrid to Thucydus 1809 Drownd in Crick Cristmas Day 1832" and the comment dated 23 June 1833, "Who in hell ever heard of a niger drownding him self" (p. 267). And the explanation, long unacknowledged, appears in the fact that the old man left a thousand dollar legacy to the son of an unmarried slave girl. The child, Terrel Beauchamp, gains a bride through the luck of Isaac's uncle who won her in a poker game: "Possible Strait against three Treys in sigt Not called 1859" (p. 271). Isaac sees all this at sixteen because he had experienced the rape of Old Ben.[18]

In part IV of "The Bear," Isaac, now twenty-one, can verbalize the tyranny: How his forefathers, reflecting the spirit of their times, grasped and held the land, making of that austere and mysterious nature God bequeathed for the enjoyment and fulfillment of man a dead thing, an oblong and square piece of property, to be passed from generation to generation.

Isaac's compassion for human failure—he sees under the white sheet of the most ruthless Ku Klux Klanner a victim "not so much of hate as of desperation and despair" (p. 291)—suggests Faulkner's own interest in man as an existential creature. He once told a college audience that he prefers the Old to the New Testament because the latter is chiefly abstract ideas and the former "is full of people, perfectly ordinary normal heroes and blackguards just like

everybody else nowadays."[14] This does not imply sympathy
for the outrageous acts of racial bigotry that Faulkner's own
novels document, but implies rather his belief that the root of
Southern bigotry calls for a more sophisticated analysis of
its social, political, and economic manifestations. Paralleling
the manipulation of property and of nature with the white
man's inhuman treatment of the Negro, Faulkner questions the
very foundations of American society. In doing so, he confesses like Heidegger that if man's exploitation of nature
has led to an impasse, a fresh perspective cannot be created
by some sort of ontological leap into new existence. Man
has not yet found a way to circumvent the conditioning that
has defined him.

 Significantly, the Biblical Isaac, one of Faulkner's
favorite characters, does not emigrate, as did his parents, but
remains in Palestine to endure the inauthenticity which
victimizes him and his fellow citizens. The novelist's choice
of names for his hero utilizes these facts. He tells us that
if Isaac McCaslin "avoided conflict, it was not because of any
cowardice but because of a trust that what he needed would
be given him from God." While the emphasis is more upon
apocalyptic faith than action, the distinction can be misleading.
Isaac's willingness to wait for God, to endure in the expectation of redemption, reflects the sort of openness many
modern writers have affirmed as a courageous act of faith. In
this regard, I have referred to what Wordsworth termed
"wise passiveness" and Keats "negative capability" as the
strength to oppose one's easier submission to a derivative
past.[15]

 Isaac overcomes the temptation to ignore his own
atrocities. Where his grandfather leaves one thousand dollars
to Terrel Beauchamp so he won't have to say "My son to
a nigger" (p. 269) or face the boredom that drove him first to
seduce the mother and then the child, Isaac struggles to
oppose this human inclination in himself.

 The white Southerner's argument that intention is no

less important than acts may strike us as an easy rationalization for status quo. There is little to suggest, however, that Faulkner became a captive of such Southern apologetics. Adopting a Biblical view of man, he cautions the liberal to consider whether the social and political liberties with which white middle-class Americans are blessed have resulted in meaningful freedom. The sad irony remains that in some important respects, the disenfranchised black appears more free than his white ruler. What does it matter, Faulkner might have asked, that all the blacks in the Mississippi Delta are registered to vote, if in the process of adopting the mores of a success-oriented society they lose their mysterious sense of being alive? James Baldwin similarly has questioned whether the blacks' salvation lies in adopting social structures the white man has established largely for himself. Faulkner, like Baldwin, suggests that perhaps it is the white man who should learn from the Negro an authenticity that the mechanical escalation of Western civilization has all but obliterated.

From sex to civil war to huckstering to Boston socializing, Faulkner describes a bourgeois society preoccupied with the limited goals that sustain its self-image. Isaac's indictment of every stratum of American society, not least "the mellifluous choiring of self-styled men of God" recalls the existential critique of a world in pursuit of forgetfulness. The Boston-bred who look "if at anything other than Beacon Hill, only toward heaven" (p. 287), the manipulators of townsites, and currency, the dedicated heroes of Cemetery Ridge and Gettysburg reveal the malaise. Their frenetic motion speaks of a refusal to step back and consider the "slogging and brutal stupidity" of war, the consuming fever of greed, the boredom of derived ritual, a failure to renounce, at least momentarily, the forces that compel them to action.

While the captives of society exist in painless obedience, the existential hero, through his courage to question the very meaning that sustains him, finds that the depth of

things appears in a new way. Meursault, the hero of Camus'
The Stranger, is aware of the consequence of his new alienation.
In the midst of firing five shots into the Arab's body, he
describes the change: "I knew I'd shattered the balance of
the day, the spacious calm of this beach on which I had been
happy."[16] With the growing threat of deprivation, Meursault's
existence assumes greater significance. The world outside
his prison cell window becomes alive: "The stars were shining
down on my face. Sounds of the countryside came faintly
in, and the cool night air, veined with smells of earth and
salt, fanned my cheeks."[17] In accepting his own guilt and his
own death, Meursault, like Camus' Sisyphus, discovers that
for the first time he cares about tomorrow and yesterday and
he understands why at the end of her life his mother became a
"fiancée." Similarly, Isaac experiences a clearer sense of
time past, present, and future. He realizes both the burden
and the advantage of his new freedom: to be, as he puts it to
his cousin, more than what he is.

Both part IV (Isaac at twenty-one) and part V (Isaac
at sixteen) reveal the hero's capacity to see others and to see
himself. In denying the static truth that his cousin defends—to
perpetuate his grandfather's name and accomplishments—
Isaac faces the chaos that accompanies his own renunciation.
Taking Cas's hypothetical argument with utmost seriousness
—"If truth is one thing to me and another thing to you, how
will we choose which is truth?"—he affirms the truth of
subjectivity: "The heart already knows" (p. 260). Such
knowledge, without humility, can easily become egocentric.
Faulkner, however, like the philosophers of existence and
their Biblical counterparts, emphasizes the virtue of awe that
characterizes authentic man's response to the mystery of
Being. Subjectivity, as we know, becomes tyranny at the
moment it ceases to marvel at the reality of other subjects.

The freedom that Isaac achieves is the possibility of
creating a name for himself through his own encounter with
Being and nothingness. Like his black relative who trans-

formed his name from Lucius to Lucas—"making it no longer the white man's but his own" (p. 281)—Isaac reconstitutes his own identity from the history that has formed him. He inherits the facts of his family history just as "Noah's grand-children had inherited the Flood" (p. 289). Isaac therefore condemns as "heresy" his own compulsion to escape the demands of history by relinquishing the tainted land that has been willed to him.

Much has been written about Isaac McCaslin's act of renunciation in part IV of "The Bear." Let me suggest further that Faulkner had no intention of isolating Isaac and affirming his renunciation as some sort of Stoic or Christian virtue. Instead, he projects his hero's future in eschatological terms. "The courage to face one's own guilt," Tillich suggests, "leads to the question of salvation instead of renunciation."[18] Implicit in Stoicism is a faith in man's courage and in his reason. The passage that Tillich quotes from Epictetus—"I have maintained that which is under my control"—makes this clear.

Isaac's virtue is manifest because he is no less pas-sion's slave than those whose conduct he laments. His sense of personal guilt makes it hard for him to escape finitude through heroic action. The closing section of part IV should be read with this point in mind. When Isaac capitulates to his wife's demand that he take the farm (the inheritance he has sought to reject), he confesses the failure that neither reason, nor courage, nor humility can finally avoid: "and he thought, *She is lost, She was born lost. We were all born lost* then he stopped thinking and even saying Yes" (pp. 314–315). The inevitability of his capitulation is as clear to Isaac as had been the death of Old Ben. To avoid his wife's intended seduction, he must deny sexuality as well as the nihilistic compulsions that had led three generations of McCaslins to escape the bondage of time. We may well ask what then remains of the hero's affirmation.

The dramatic reversal in "The Bear," like Uncle Ike's

own attack upon the black mother in "Delta Autumn," defies
all expectation of easy progress. For Faulkner it is finally
only through faith that the future (whether by some Eternal
Being's intervention or a shifting pattern of social forces) may
be sought as potentially redemptive. At an early point in
the boy's life, one of the hunters, General Compson, recognizes
the virtues that distinguished Isaac from his relatives:
"You've got one foot straddled into a farm and the other foot
straddled into a bank," he shouts at Cas Edmonds. "You
aint even got a good hand-hold where this boy was already
an old man long before you damned Sartorises and Edmondses
invented farms and banks to keep yourselves from having
to find out what this boy was born knowing" (p. 250). What
Compson decrees to be "the why and wherefores of farms
and banks" is simply Isaac's determination to encounter the
bear. For this reason he passes on to Isaac the silver mounted
horn at that very time when everyone has taken for granted
that the boy has "quit." This central narrative act, rooted
in both a mythic and a Biblical tradition, unifies the closing
chapters of *Go Down, Moses.*

Horns, long associated with power and divinity,
appear equally in pagan and Judeo-Christian conceptions of
deity. The Hebrew word for horn *(geren),* emphasizing
the exaltation of that self capable of resisting tyranny, is seen
throughout the Old Testament in relation both to news and
to kingship.[19] At one time, many people held that Moses
actually had horns growing from his head. Later, the horn was
associated with Christ (II Samuel 22:3, "horn of my salvation"). In addition to that connotation of power drawn from
the picture of horned beasts, there exists a more gentle
meaning derived, perhaps, from the sense of *cornucopia*
(abundance), or the more familiar image of "the horn
of plenty."

Through Faulkner's art, the horn becomes an
effective means of conveying the ambivalence of being in
the world. The source of the hunter's horns are the very deer

whose life and death sustain his activity. He must take up
the beast's horn and, like the poet, recreate the sublimity
he has encountered (halted). The callous hunter collects
antlers as a sign of his prowess, hanging his musket on the
horns as if in proud recognition of the domination of life
by cold, man-forged metal. But such are the nameless men
who live together in herds, in order, Faulkner suggests,
to protect themselves from their own sources of life. Like the
dogs who responded first to Sam's horn, swarming around
the fallen buck to get a taste of the blood, such men seek
to devour the land and with it themselves. When Sam bathes
Isaac in the blood, he initiates his mythical son into the awe-
some ritual through which reverence is paid to the being
that, through no choice of his own, man is born to hunt and to
kill. Paradoxically then, the horn in *Go Down, Moses*
announces the death of deer and of bear while through Sam
Fathers and then Isaac McCaslin it represents the kingship of
those who would preserve a revelatory sense of life.

Shortly after Isaac's initiation, the hunting party,
excited by the report that another large deer is in the area, sets
out in pursuit. When Isaac and Sam hear the single report of
Walter Ewell's rifle—the hunter who never missed—and "then
the mellow sound of the horn" (p. 183), Isaac feels an
empty disappointment, as if the experience that so recently
inspired him was now abruptly ended. Faulkner's stress
upon the mellowness of Ewell's report carries with it a sense
of gentle termination that clashes with the expectancy of
youth. Turning toward his old teacher, Isaac is surprised to
see him looking through him toward the sounding horn. At
that moment, he sees the gigantic buck "coming down the
ridge, as if it were walking out of the very sound of the
horn which related its death." Taller than any man, the buck's
antlers fill him once again with a sense of grandeur. This time
he does not shoot, although the beast, its head high, passes
within twenty feet of the two hunters. Sam, like a priest
before deity, raises his arm, palm outward, speaking in a

strange tongue the boy had sometimes heard him use. Then
the half-Indian, half-Negro pronounces those words that Isaac
himself will repeat in the closing section of "The Bear":
" 'Oleh, Chief,' Sam said. 'Grandfather' " (p. 184). His
tribute, in contrast to the sound of Ewell's horn "'blowing them
into a dead buck," affirms a holiness at the ground of Being
that Faulkner's novel seeks to disclose.

The other hunters seem unable to see the buck.
Desiring to seek out and destroy the animal they fail to open
themselves to the mystery of the wilderness. When the boy
relates the story to his cousin, the latter confesses that
once, shortly after his own first kill, Sam had taken him into
that secret spot and there the buck had also appeared to
him. Cas centers the experience in a time past, during that
moment of innocent childhood when such images could
elicit belief. We realize how much the older man has
already relinquished.

With the death of Sam Fathers and the loss of those
true hunters like Compson and De Spain, Isaac must take up
the mantle of prophet. Through Sam he has received the
mysterious spirit of kingship, and through General Compson
the no less important historical tradition in which spirit
is manifest.

The silver horn that Compson passes on to Isaac
stands in relationship to another legacy that Isaac receives from
his godfather and uncle, Hubert Beauchamp: a silver cup,
formerly filled with gold pieces, wrapped in burlap and sealed
with wax. From his earliest days Isaac remembers his uncle
unlocking the closet and taking down this weighty
representation of the link between generations, the legacy
through which an old man though close to death could still
derive significance. The family had sanctified the examination
of the cup. Seated around the table, each member received
the sacrament: Beauchamp, "passing it from hand to hand: his
mother, his father, McCaslin and even Tennie, insisting
that each take it in turn and heft it for weight and shake

it again to prove the sound." Then, after a long period of time, the young boy remembers that his uncle would take down the cup and give it only to him, standing over him until he had obediently shaken it and "until it sounded" (p. 304).

This legacy, with its obvious reference to the gold and silver idols that Moses decried, has corrupted each generation of McCaslins. The silver cup, filled first with gold coins and then finally with coppers and I.O.U.s, was to supply substance to the inheritor. Its sound, first the substantial ring of gold against silver and finally the muted rattling of copper against tin, is proof of a promise that would give Isaac the power necessary to control the land and thereby continue the history his forefathers had established and decreed for him. As he tells his cousin, however, Sam and the wilderness have set him free. Like the Hebrew predecessors for whom he was named, Isaac adopts Compson's horn as the symbol of his new life. (The phrase "to lift up the horn" is relevant.) In "Delta Autumn," now as Uncle Ike, his decision is dramatized. The act of passing on this silver horn to his black relative takes meaning from that central incident anticipated in "The Old People" and revealed in "The Bear."

When old Isaac accompanies the younger hunters to the Delta country, he witnesses the inevitable repetition of that betrayal he had faced earlier in his life. Roth Edmonds, grandson of McCaslin Edmonds, before departing to hunt, leaves an envelope filled with money on Isaac's cot. He asks the old man to give it to a girl who will come to their camp and to "tell her no." The visitor, a black woman with whom Roth has fathered a child, turns out to be the granddaughter of Tennie's Jim, taking her ancestral line, like Roth's, back to Isaac's grandfather.

The mother enters the tent with a child in her arms. She recognizes "Uncle Isaac" at once. When he offers her the money, she turns away with a look that strikes him as "incredibly and even ineradicably alive," and then chastises the old man for having contributed to the moral decline of her lover by giving "'his grandfather [Cas] that land which didn't belong to him" (p. 360).

In despair over this familiar turn of events and confronted once again with the futility of his own efforts to change or even modify the pattern, he asks what she hopes to accomplish by her presence. Her reply—"nothing"—increases his suffering. Crying out "in that thin not loud and grieving voice" (that recalls the plaintive wailing of Old Ben) he tells her to leave: "Get out of here! I can do nothing for you! Cant nobody do nothing for you!" She refuses the money with the confession "I don't need it" (p. 361). He pleads with her to take the tainted envelope out of his tent so he will no longer have to face the sign of his own iniquity. Apparently moved by his inability to face a reality three generations of McCaslins had ignored she takes the money and starts to leave the tent.

At this moment of the narrative, Isaac recovers the strength that has made him a hero. Asking her to wait, he extends his gnarled old hand toward the young girl's hand in a gesture that recalls Michelangelo's Sistine Jehovah: "He touched it. He didn't grasp it, he merely touched it—the gnarled, bloodless, bone-light bone-dry old man's fingers touching for a second the smooth young flesh where the strong old blood ran after its long lost journey back to home. 'Tennie's Jim' he said" (p. 362). In that instant the barriers of race and of the past are suspended if not banished. Although he cannot say "my son" to a "nigger," he does more. Directing the mother to a nail on the tent pole he asks her to bring down the silver horn and offers it for the child: "It's his. Take it." Then, the moment past, he relapses into a present without depth. His voice "running away with him . . . he had neither intended it nor could stop it," Isaac finds himself bound to the life that has conditioned him. Telling her that she will have to wait, he counsels her, as would any proper Southern bigot, to marry a black man and "forget all this,

forget it ever happened, that he ever existed." Having passed
the symbol of new life to his only "son," his submission,
like Lear's "defeat," signifies the tragic consequence of finitude.

Looking quietly down at him from outside his tent in
the morning rain, the black mother pronounces the sad
question Isaac knows to be true: " 'Old Man,' she said, 'have
you lived so long and forgotten so much that you dont
remember anything you ever knew or felt or even heard
about love?' " (p. 363). She leaves him lying corpse-like under
the blanket, listening to the motor of her departing boat
and finally only to the sound of rain.

Isaac's life is over, but in that moment with his black
cousin he has been grasped by a meaning that has grown
from his own tangled history. Decision as well as fate seem
involved. The cold knowledge of cyclical inevitability cannot
destroy the "care" through which Faulkner's hero looks in
expectation toward a future that has evaded him. His suffering
gives further testimony that Faulkner views man as something more than the social forces that have formed
his consciousness.

In passing the horn to his black descendants, Isaac
McCaslin has not changed the course of that history he
inherited as a young man. But, like the Biblical Isaac, he has
handed on to his children the sign of life's potential fullness.
As decreed in Jacob's dream, this inheritance shall transform
the human community:

> And thy seed shall be as the dust of the earth,
> and thou shalt spread abroad to the west, and to
> the east, and to the north, and to the south: and in
> thee and in thy seed shall all the families of the
> earth be blessed. (Genesis 28:14)

If there is to be hope, Faulkner tells us, it must come
from those who, enduring history, can exist as intruders in
the dust. His next novel looks, with no less prophetic
intention, to black America to keep the faith.

The black narrator of Ralph Ellison's novel, *Invisible Man*, allows himself to be drawn by often mysterious compulsions toward an apparently impractical course of action. Paradoxically, the impulse to turn off the familiar highway (with its unambiguous "white line") when chauffeuring Norton, the rich white trustee of his college, leads Invisible Man both to his expulsion from school and, as Ellison puts it elsewhere, "to run the risk of his own humanity."[1] Before his debilitating experience with Norton, he had adhered with comic naiveté to "the rightness of things as they are." Following a savage and humiliating ordeal in the white man's smoker, the young high school student passively accepts the scholarship from his white benefactors as proof that Southern society takes care of its own.

At the black college his confidence in things as they are continued unchallenged. But, looking back, he can question: "What was real, what solid" in those recollections where "honeysuckle and purple wisteria hung heavy from the trees and white magnolias mixed with their scents in the bee-humming air?" Success there depended upon the mind's willingness to accept the sensuous pictures of well-being and remain the passive inmate of a "flower-studded wasteland."[2] So long as the black man privileged to be a student viewed the future in terms imposed by the trustees of his consciousness, black as well as white, happiness was assured.

The "meaning" Invisible Man encounters and presumes during his picaresque journey through American society is rooted in hierarchical presuppositions. From his first unwitting blunder, when he stutters out the word "equality" rather than "responsibility" while reading his graduation speech after the "battle royal," through his experiences with Bledsoe in college and the officials of the Brotherhood in New York, he learns the hard lesson that "sense" is equated with the subjugation of self and the priority of "place." As the master of ceremonies instructs the boy following his error at

the smoker: "you had better speak more slowly so we can
understand. We mean to do right by you, but you've got
to know your place at all times" (p. 25). The instruction, with
its emphasis upon understanding, reward, and self-abnegation,
represents far more than the sociological implications of
white racism. It reflects, as we shall see, Ellison's response
to a major direction of Western thought. At the close of the
novel, the perceptive reader no longer dismisses such
exploitation (in the white liberal tradition) as the result of
unenlightened leadership or the failure of American
education. The unattractive assumptions stated so crassly
by the white Southern bigot are operative principles of that
larger environment which has formed us all.

As I have suggested, the narrator must learn that
self-examination takes priority over social protest.[3] Like
Faulkner, Ellison moves relentlessly through distortion and
subterfuge toward the sources of that meaning which defines
his visibility. The hero's movement downward in the novel,
metaphorically and literally, is paradoxically "a process
of *rising*," as Ellison explains in *Shadow and Act*, "to an
understanding of his human condition." The concluding scene
is significantly not a sewer but a coal cellar: "a source of
heat, light, power and, through association with the character's
motivation, self-perception."[4]

To exchange the well-defined values of an operative
white power structure for some dark and obscure vision of
existential significance may imply either the courage or,
antithetically, the stupidity to deny "sense." Error, however,
is not the sole consequence of non-sense. Razumihin's
affirmation of nonsense in *Crime and Punishment* contributes to the expanded meaning Ellison has in mind: "Talk
nonsense, but talk your own nonsense, and I'll kiss you for
it . . . Truth won't escape you, but life can be cramped."
Understood in these terms, Invisible Man gains the possibility
of new meaning as a consequence of leaving the safe highway.
The uncharted dirt road carries Norton and the student

chauffeur to Jim Trueblood, a poor black sharecropper,
infamous in the college community for having fathered his
daughter's child. Through this outcast, Ellison offers the
first model for his hero's more authentic education.

The wealthy trustee, who has endowed the black
college largely in memory of his daughter, confronts Trueblood
with incredulous surprise: "You have looked upon chaos and
are not destroyed!" (p. 40). The black replies with a comic
resignation which only further upsets the white man. At
Norton's insistence he tells his story, a meandering narrative
filled with reminiscences of his former life on the river. His
description of these former incidents—listening to the sounds
of the river boat, watching the gentle movement of its lights
on the water, hunting quail at evening when their whistling
fills the growing silence of dusk—overshadows the particulars
of his transgression. Trueblood's response to existence
infuses inanimate matter with life. Such awareness is not
solely impressionistic. Recognizing his own helplessness before
the injustice of man and the amorality of nature, he explains
the conditions that gave rise to the incest: "I couldn't find
no work or nothin! It was so cold all of us had to sleep
together; me, the ole lady and the gal. That's how it started,
suh" (p. 42). The comic aspects of his dilemma, awakening
to find that the sexual fantasy of his dream had somehow
become the reality of his daughter's body, effectively conveys a
rather heavily worked literary theme: the futility of man's
efforts before an unbending universe.

Trueblood is no Ancient Mariner compelled to relate
his iniquity. But, as with Coleridge's narrator, an expansion
of consciousness helps him to endure the disruption of order.
Ellison affirms this heroic quality on existential grounds.

Trueblood's primitive innocence resembles the
simplicity of Rose in *Brighton Rock*. Both commit acts that are
anathema to their respective societies, and both thereby
achieve a new sense of independence and responsibility. Trueblood "ends up singin' the blues." Returning to his family,

he does not flee from the consequences of his actions. In confessing, "I ain't nobody but myself" (p. 51), the old farmer awakens from the nightmare which he has recounted. Norton, whose incestuous desires for his own daughter remain largely unconscious, exists in a state of somnambulism. His activity as benefactor of the Southern Negro only masks the source of such passion. Ellison's point, however, is not directed solely at Norton; it applies to all strata of society and particularly to his own protagonist, who still clings with quiet desperation to the only order he has been lucky enough to experience. At this stage of his education, Invisible Man, like the black college officials, looks upon the primitive True-blood with shame; when the sharecropper reaches out compassionately to put his hand on the boy's shoulder, the latter draws back in revulsion. Fearing that Trueblood's uncivilized tale has disrupted his rapport with the influential trustee, he sees the sharecropper solely within the framework of this narrow and largely uncritical intention.

Bledsoe, the Uncle Tom college president, is furious at the student for allowing Norton to see what he had never intended him to see. Ironically, by comparison with Trueblood, neither Bledsoe, Norton, nor the narrator is capable of seeing anything but projections of their own limited sense of reality. "The vet," another estranged character who enters the narrative during the Trueblood incident, sums up their myopia while attending to Norton in the Golden Day Saloon: "Poor stumblers, neither of you can see the other. To you he is a mark on the score-card of your achievement, a thing and not a man; a child, or even less—a black amorphous thing. And you, for all your power, are not a man to him, but a God, a force—" (p. 73).

The veteran, himself an inmate of an asylum for shell-shocked black war veterans, meets the narrator again on the bus after the latter's dismissal from school. His advice, echoing Trueblood's, is more explicit: "Be your own father, young man. And remember, the world is possibility if only

you'll discover it. Last of all, leave the Mr. Nortons alone, and
if you don't know what I mean, think about it" (p. 120).
When the vet disembarks, however, Invisible Man is happy
to see him gone. Still committed to hierarchical morality, he
leaves for New York with the expectation that Bledsoe's sealed
letters of reference will enable him through good works to
atone for his sin and return to college. But by advising each
prospective employer against hiring him, Bledsoe makes
use of the student's naive faith to dispose of a potential
troublemaker.

  The end of the protagonist's formal education
signals the beginning of his inner life. Deprived of the pleasant
pattern of college routine, the problem of his future ceases
to be academic. The disturbing questions—"Where would I go,
what could I do? How could I ever return home?" (p. 104)
—reveal that the hero's education has in fact begun.

  Invisible Man's desire to be free of past inequity
leads him to new forms of bondage. As a worker in the Liberty
Paint Factory and then as a member of the Brotherhood
in New York City, he finds how strongly his own need
"to be accepted" requires the paternalism he just rejected.
The narrator must suffer the demise of these self-destructive
compulsions before rising to understand himself. The choice to
live, in existential terms, requires the willingness to begin
as well as the courage to resist annihilation.

  While Ellison appears to abide by Razumihin's
axiom—"I am a man because I err!"—he places high priority
on "mind" when establishing his own sense of the authentic
life. The self that grows into self-examination is the self
capable of reflection. Society's appropriation of "thought,"
however, confronts the narrator with an important contradiction. Admonishing Invisible Man for upsetting Norton,
Bledsoe confesses that he had considered him "a boy with
brains," in other words, a student who could follow orders.
His idea of education, predicated on a notion of power which
circumvents the life of the mind, claims the sanction of

Six Existential Heroes

both thought and practicality: "You let white folks worry
about pride and dignity—you learn where you are and get your-
self power, influence, contacts with powerful and influential
people—then stay in the dark and use it!" (p. 111).

College mirrors the society that surrounds it.
Invisible Man discovers Bledsoe's dogma wherever he turns.
At the Liberty Paint Factory his first foreman instructs him
in the ways of the world: "Just do what you're told and don't
try to think about it" (p. 152). In the hospital infirmary,
following the paint explosion, he tells the doctors that he
cannot feel his head. The chief surgeon, delighted with the
result of his therapy, replies: "You see! My little gadget
will solve everything!" (p. 179). Brother Jack, under the banner
of "science" and "party discipline" reprimands Invisible
Man for making a personal decision: "You were not hired to
think" (p. 355). Hambro, the party theoretician, like Mary
Rambo, and the manufacturers of Sambo dolls, all express the
paternalism, or in Mary's case, maternalism, that denies
Invisible Man the dignity of thought.

In each case Ellison indirectly equates authentic
existence with the mind's capacity to question and deny the
validity of that meaning in which it participates. Paul Tillich,
describing this human possibility as the capacity to raise
"ontological questions," speaks of man in this regard as "free
to transcend every given reality."[5] Through shock treatment,
the infirmary doctors try to obliterate precisely this capacity
of the narrator's mind. Ironically, their treatment inadvertently
motivates the very doubt and disquietude they hoped to
remove. Once all the memories of the names he has received
from others are shaken out of him, Invisible Man finds he has
only one source of identity left, the center of consciousness
that must ask the question: "Who am I?" (p. 183).

Ellison's description of the nurse clipping the belly
band that connects Invisible Man to his mechanical womb
(the hospital machine) conveys, rather laboriously, this new
sense of significance in terms of birth. When the newly born

hero emerges into Harlem from the depths of the subway,
however, the novelist's language is strikingly effective.
Invisible Man sees Lenox Avenue "with wild infant's eyes."
Like the existential perception discussed in *Mrs. Dalloway*,
this personal vision is both dynamic and frightening. Objects
and people can no longer be safely assimilated in terms of
abstractly derived meaning. They must be encountered. The
identification of phenomena, bound up as it is with the
individual's new sense of inwardness, includes an expanded
sense of urgency. The black women who first enter Invisible
Man's sight appear like figures from a Renoir canvas: "Two
huge women with spoiled-cream complexions seemed to
struggle with their massive bodies as they came past, their
flowered hips trembling like threatening flames" (p. 191).
Ready to explode into impermanence, their flashing presence
testifies in some strange manner to both the tentativeness and
the uniqueness of Being. The urgency that characterizes such
vision imbues the scene with strikingly modern significance.

Growing in self-knowledge, the protagonist
discovers a corresponding sense of vitality in the familiar
objects that surround him. Almost simultaneously, he admits
the tension that results from his own freedom and his new
and more personal involvement with the world: "the obsession
with my identity which I had developed in the factory
hospital returned with a vengeance. Who was I, how had I
come to be? Certainly I couldn't help being different from
when I left the campus; but now a new, painful, contradictory
voice had grown up within me" (p. 197). Contradiction is a
definitive experience for the existential hero. For Invisible
Man, no less than for Clarissa Dalloway or Isaac McCaslin,
human freedom includes the individual's willingness to
endure such dissonance.

Witnessing the eviction of the old black couple in
Harlem, he hears the white mover plead with the crowd that
he is being forced to displace them: "They sent me up here
to do it" (p. 204). The surrounding crowd, of which Invisible

Six Existential Heroes

Man is part, picks up the impersonal "they" as the safe and
distant perpetuators of injustice. The abstraction, a source of
self-pity, removes the necessity of any act:

> "Don't tell me," she said. "It's all the white folks,
> not just one. They all against us. Every stinking
> low-down one of them."
> "She's right!" a hoarse voice said. "She's right!
> They *all* is!"

Invisible Man, suddenly aware that he and the others are in
fact ashamed of witnessing the eviction, admits "we were
careful not to touch or stare too hard at the effects that lined
the curb; for we were witnesses of what we did not wish
to see" (p. 205).

As he stares at the junk piled in front of the tenement
—discarded trinkets, broken-down furniture, souvenirs from
a life of bondage and restricted opportunity—the worthless
bric-a-brac all throb within him "with more meaning than there
should have been . . . far beyond their intrinsic meaning as
objects" (p. 207). Forced, like Isaac, to look into the conditions
of that history inherited from a past he has been unwilling
to face, the narrator appears to see these details for the first
time; his descriptions recall Trueblood's remembrance of life
on the river. But now it is the narrator who is involved in
the objects that make up his experience.

Kierkegaard suggests repeatedly that freedom
"exists" only in so far as it becomes "something." Paradoxically, in becoming something, the free act sets in motion
the conditions that will determine its demise. Man, caught
in the dialectic between possibility and necessity, must remain
conscious of the contradiction. "If he is to recover his
freedom," Kierkegaard suggests, "it can only be through an
intensified 'fear and trembling' brought forth by the thought
of having lost it."[6]

Invisible Man's greatest temptation to find security

in a derivative existence occurs at those very moments when he experiences possibility. The reason is plain. The consequence of stepping back from the surrounding environment is the disturbing experience Kierkegaard called "objective uncertainty." Revolutionary politics (the Brotherhood) offers Invisible Man the vocational means of translating his dangling existence into concrete social action and thereby of silencing "the contradictory voice" within him. What he cannot see at the time is the appeal of anesthetizing those dangerous compulsions that have led him to existential doubt. When on the streets of Harlem his new friend Tod Clifton confesses that there are times when a man feels compelled to plunge outside history, Invisible Man cannot answer him: "Maybe he's right, I thought, and was suddenly very glad I had found Brotherhood" (p. 285).

Ellison stresses his protagonist's failure to realize that in turning from contradiction he has allowed others to name him once again. The scrap of paper he accepts from Brother Jack with his new name written on it, and his decision to submit uncritically to party discipline, express his new submission to the intentions of others. His thoughts about Mary Rambo reveal how he has agreed to see as others have determined he should see: "Even if I met Mary on the street, I'd have to pass her by unrecognized" (p. 254).

The narrator's loyalty, like his former submission to Bledsoe, contributes to the calamity that follows. Accepting Brother Jack's apparently unreasonable command some months later to leave Harlem and lecture downtown on the woman question, Invisible Man unwittingly facilitates the party's decision to sacrifice the black community. Without a leader, all organization collapses. When he returns for a visit, the Brotherhood office is deserted; even Tod Clifton, his most dedicated associate, has disappeared from Harlem.

By chance, Invisible Man discovers his friend selling Black Sambo dolls to a crowd of amused white people in midtown Manhattan. Clifton's new job recalls the night he had confessed his temptation to plunge outside of history. The empty Sambo dolls, dancing mechanically on the hot city pavement, symbolize the consequence of Clifton's desertion. The scene's climax occurs some moments later when a policeman, incited by Clifton's resistance to arrest, shoots him dead before the crowd of onlookers. Plagued by the question—"Why did he choose to plunge into nothingness . . . ?" (p. 331)—Invisible Man suppresses the thought that his own apparent defection might have motivated Clifton's loss of faith. As long as the hero believes that his existence has no validity apart from the Brotherhood's "historical" intentions, he can withstand guilt with the delusion that "the incident was political" (p. 337).

Clifton's funeral and the eulogy Invisible Man delivers there weaken these rationalizations. As he moves with the crowd of mourners toward the hill where the burial will take place, intent to win back Harlem for what he naively believes is the good of the Brotherhood, a number of questions distract his political intentions. Why does Harlem turn out in such large numbers for a man unknown to the vast majority of the mourners? "Did it signify love or politicized hate? . . . Could politics ever be an expression of love?" (p. 341). While climbing to the muffled sound of drums, the melodious singing of a masculine voice moves the procession to join in the singing. The narrator is suddenly aware that something mysteriously more important than protest or religion has touched every one of them: "Deepened by that something for which the theory of Brotherhood had given [him] no name" (p. 342), he finds the purpose of his funeral oration transformed. The unexpected intrusion of personal feelings brings to mind that moment during his first formal speech when, forgetting the ideology of Brotherhood, he suddenly confessed to the crowd that he had become more human.[7]

Like Hamlet's soliloquies, the narrator's speeches reveal his internal development. The "battle royal" address initiated the high school student into a white man's world

which only the deepest part of his psyche dared question.
When, under the badgering of his white audience, he had said
"equality" instead of "responsibility" he quickly rectified
his error; within the framework of a white Southern community the confusion between the two concepts eliminated freedom
of choice. The capacity for social protest began with the
second oration outside the Harlem tenement, followed by the
auditorium speech where he first verbalized his new sense of
identity. Now, Invisible Man, confronted by Clifton's coffin,
must recreate life in the face of death; the only thing he can
remember of the deceased, he tells the silent audience, is
"the sound of his name." His eulogy is a testimony to the
holiness of Being revealed in that name.

      The recurring refrain, "His name was Clifton," is
linked by a Brotherhood member to Mark Antony's oration
over the body of Caesar. Whereas Brutus, however, sought to
move the crowd to his intentions by rhetoric, the narrator
endeavors, through his description of Clifton's life and death,
to spur each member of the crowd to a sense of personal
responsibility both for the murder and for maintaining the
hopes that Tod Clifton's presence had aroused before his
death. Significantly, when he turns at the close to take one last
look at the scene, Invisible Man speaks of seeing "not a
crowd but the set faces of individual men and women" (p. 347).

      The speaker, comparing Clifton's murder with the
crucifixion of Jesus, establishes the former as a sacrilege on
all that is holy in life. The "official" execution, uncontested by
the crowd, characterizes both historical events. Invisible
Man's sarcastic advice for the assembly to forget the murdered
one attempts to drive each listener to face his particular
unwillingness to bring their highest ideals (represented in
the name "Clifton") into history through courage and
through faith:[8] "go home, keep cool, stay safe away from the
sun. Forget him. When he was alive he was our hope, but why
worry over a hope that's dead? So there's only one thing
left to tell and I've already told it. His name was Tod Clifton,

he believed in Brotherhood, he aroused our hopes and
he died" (p. 346).

The passage recalls W. H. Auden's ridicule of
bourgeois Christianity in *For the Time Being* as well as the
prose passage to which Ellison refers in a relevant essay,
"Hidden Name and Complex Fate." Auden, characterizing
the twentieth century as an age that would make a work of art
a political act, urges the artist to resist "the Management."
Managers, he goes on to say, need to be reminded by the
artist "that the managed are people with faces, not anonymous
members." Ellison extends Auden's statement about the
managed to include people with names. The essay, as if in
explication of the section of *Invisible Man* just discussed,
asserts the magic of our hidden names.[9]

Brother Jack's attack on the narrator's unwillingness
to be managed is expanded by Brother Hambro's subsequent
discourse on "realism." The Brotherhood's credo is based
upon a thesis of unavoidable manipulation: "It's impossible
not to take advantage of the people," the party theoretician
tells his disillusioned student; "the trick is to take advantage
of them in their own best interests" (p. 381). Invisible Man,
increasingly aware that his presence is of little importance, asks
who is to make this determination, and Hambro obligingly
responds that the Brotherhood judges by cultivating a
"scientific objectivity." Party discipline seeks to objectify the
hero in a manner similar to his exploitation at the smoker,
the black college, and the paint factory.

Just prior to this last visit with Hambro, Invisible
Man, fleeing from the militant black nationalist named Ras the
exhorter, disguises himself by wearing a large-brimmed hat
and sun glasses. In this attire he is mistaken for Rinehart,
a Harlem gambler, woman's man and professional preacher.
The unintended deception tempts him to give up the disturbing
question of his identity: "If dark glasses and a white hat
could blot out my identity so quickly," he speculates while
disguised as Rinehart, "who actually was who?" (p. 373).

When Hambro offers his doctrine of manipulation as an alternative to personal dignity, however, the hero replies angrily: "That's Rinehartism—cynicism—" (p. 381).

Hambro's warning that his pupil's defense of individual autonomy will destroy all confidence in political action leads Invisible Man once again to doubt. If others do not supply the authority for action, how, the Party tutor insists, can the individual ever find the assurance within himself necessary to lead others? The hero is being led to an important impasse. Stopping after the interview to sit on a park bench, he realizes the frightening absence of any meaningful alternative to Bledsoe, Hambro, or Rinehart. To move from one to the other meant jumping "from the pot of absurdity to the fire of the ridiculous" (p. 382). There follows an incident reminiscent of the scene we have discussed in Sartre's novel *Nausea*.

Like Ellison's Invisible Man, Sartre's narrator encounters nothingness on a park bench: the realization that "every existing thing is born without reason, prolongs itself out of weakness and dies by chance." Against such absurdity only one reality stubbornly asserts itself. Roquentin, responding initially to the obscene nakedness of the chestnut tree, questions everything before finding an alternative in his own reaction to nothing.

Brother Jack had shocked the narrator when, in the midst of their argument, he plopped his glass eye into a tumbler of water. Seated in the park, Invisible Man's recollection of amorphous rawness between the leader's eyelids occasions a dread similar to Roquentin's. Both narrators, perceiving that form is a tenuous mask upon the faceless features of cosmic anarchy, find only one affirmation left to them. Even the metaphysical blank that underlay political institutions such as the Brotherhood, the narrator confesses, "was without meaning except for me."

But what "meaning" does such awareness infer? Invisible Man expresses his identity in thoroughly subjective terms—"I was and yet I was unseen." As he is seated there, the formless shadows that underlie his thoughts and acts reveal "another frightening world of possibilities," symbolized, it is true, by Rinehart's dictum that everything is permitted. Like Isaac, now that he has begun to recognize his own darkness Invisible Man makes an important decision: "I'd accept it, I'd explore it, rine and heart" (pp. 383–384).

One critic, asserting the negative quality of Ellison's metaphor, points with some consistency to Rinehart ("the incarnation of invisibility") as the actual though unintended hero of the novel.[10] Such an assumption, however, typifies the general failure of critics to deal with the ontological aspects of nothingness.

Ralph Ellison, in a symposium on the novel, describes the critic as a man driven "to create systems of thought," where the novelist, risking the unknown, plays "with the fires of chaos." Similarly, Martin Heidegger suggests that the widening gulf between criticism and art has resulted in part from the failure of the former discipline to consider the inseparable relationship of Being and nothingness. Ellison's praise of Saul Bellow helps define the achievement commentators often minimize in *Invisible Man*. Through invisibility his hero gains "a big conception of human possibility . . . informed by a knowledge of chaos which would have left the novelists of the twenties discouraged."[11] He might have added "critics" of the last few decades.

Although Invisible Man conceives of absurdity during his experience on the park bench, it is in the last section of the novel (the Harlem riot) that he experiences nothingness as the existential condition of being alive. The narrator describes the descent from Morningside Heights into the riotous darkness of Harlem as his culminating effort to run from himself. "Running from the birds to what, I didn't know. I ran. Why was I here at all?" The pigeons fluttering above his head like an image of death dramatize the hero's symbolic flight from life as well as death. The chapter ends with undefined motion: "I ran through the night, ran within myself. Ran" (p. 403).

Plunging into a social anarchy that mirrors the state of his own mind, Invisible Man wanders like a sleepwalker from street to street. Dazed by a policeman's stray bullet, he is helped by two looters, Dupre and Scofield, who enlist his aid in burning down an old tenement building.

Like Rinehart, they break the law; Ellison, however, views their decision as a free and a moral act. "You wouldn't fix it up," Scofield shouts at his mythical landlord as the tenement is consumed in flames, "now see how you like it." No more children will die of TB in this death trap. This black, "a type of man," Invisible Man speculates, which "nothing in my life had taught me to see, to understand, or respect," fulfills a threat he had made for some time. The narrator watches the flaming building with a sense of exhaltation: "They've done it, I thought. They organized it and carried it through alone; the decision their own and their own action. Capable of their own action" (pp. 413–414).

Ellison's respect for their courage, however, is not romantically uncritical. If Scofield and Dupre are ethically justified, the narrator quickly turns to a less persuasive example of self-expression. Ras the exhorter, relieved through the riot of those restraints that control his actions, becomes Ras the Abyssinian destroyer. In urging his followers to a course of thoughtless action, he becomes a tool of those very white forces he seeks to destroy. In Ras's exploitation, the narrator reads the sad consequences of his own submission.

The absurdity of two blacks fulfilling their lives by burning down their only home and of a wild black man playing the part of an African Don Quixote inspires Invisible Man with a sense of comic beauty. The revelation that their "beautiful absurdity" is also his own occasions the hero's transcendence: "I looked at Ras on his horse . . . and recognized the absurdity of the whole night and of the simple yet confoundingly complex arrangement of hope and desire, fear and hate, that had brought me here still running, and knowing now who I was and where I was and knowing too that I had no longer to run for or from the Jacks and the Emersons and the Bledsoes and Nortons, but only from their confusion, impatience, and refusal to recognize the beautiful absurdity of their American identity and mine." "I knew," he reflects, "that it was better to live out one's own absurdity than to die for that of others, whether for Ras's or Jack's" (p. 422).

Invisible Man's own rejection of the law by leaping into a coal cellar is the only way short of death in which he can maintain respect for his liberated personality. The two white policemen, peering through the manhole, demand to know who he is, which is to say: what has he concealed in his briefcase? From below, the hero replies, "all of you." The papers (things) within the case represent his former visibility. One by one he burns the articles, his high school diploma, the Black Sambo doll he took from the street when Clifton was shot, the anonymous letter he had received while in Harlem, and finally the slip of paper with his Brotherhood name written on it. When the last flame from the last article burns his hand he realizes in pain that nothing is left but himself. Alone within a series of dark and seemingly dimensionless compartments, all passion spent, he hovers in a state between dreaming and waking, "like Trueblood's jaybird that yellow jackets had paralyzed in every part but his eyes" (p. 429).

One ordeal remains; he must confront the unconscious memories of his past. Exhausted by the struggle to escape darkness, Invisible Man falls asleep to dream that he is by a black river with an armored bridge, surrounded by all those who have "run" him. When he resists their demand to recant, the crowd castrates him, tossing his genitals out over the waters where they "catch beneath the apex of the curving arch of the bridge." Brother Jack, pointing to Invisible Man's "seed wasting upon the air," ridicules the hero's effort to distinguish his own reality from the illusory identity that others have created for him: "Now," he sneers, his words recalling Hambro's final argument, "you're free of illusions." The comically grotesque nightmare continues as the iron bridge, suddenly animated by the hero's organs, becomes an apocalyptic robot, clanging "doomfully" over the waters. Free of his tormentors' intentions, Invisible Man can ridicule the monstrosity that has resulted from their "scientific" manipulation of nature: "There's your universe, and that drip drop upon the water you hear is all the history you've made, all you're going to make." Then struggling with sorrow and pain to prevent their bizarre creation from entering history, the protagonist awakens to a sense of rejuvenation: "In spite of the dream," he affirms, "I was whole" (pp. 429–431).

The past is history. Invisible Man can return to it only "from the outside." But now he is free to remain in the present, "underground," or to "move ahead." Like Wordsworth in his autobiographical poem, Ellison has recorded the prelude to an artist's future, or more appropriately, the growth of a novelist's mind. In both cases, "the end was in the beginning" (p. 431), and the beginning was in the end. The novel, however, is not over. Far from an apologia, the epilogue, organically part of the narrative that has preceded it, is in one sense the narrator's culminating oration. While reechoing a theme of personal fulfillment—"my problem was that I always tried to go in everyone's way but my own" (p. 433) —the epilogue promises less private forms of existential commitment. "In spite of all" (the threat in dream and reality), Invisible Man affirms, "I find that I love" (p. 437). The future that such self-affirmation will take remains a question that Ellison feels criticism cannot answer; such forms must be approached "from the inside," through the creative involvement the artist has achieved with his world.

Ellison's narrator is no less an artist than the young hero of Joyce's *Portrait*. Both have freed themselves from a derivative life by daring to forge the uncreated conscience of their race. But unlike Stephen Dedalus, Invisible Man shuns exile. His decision to emerge from hibernation and reenter the society that has enslaved him is an act of heroic consequence. "Life is to be lived, not controlled; and humanity is won by continuing to play in face of certain defeat" (p. 435), the narrator asserts with an absurd confidence familiar to the reader of Kierkegaard.[12] His mind, uncomfortably aware of the distinction between faith and idolatry, maintains its freedom from dogma. The capacity to question and transcend the firmest convictions of science and fantasy alike characterizes his invisible virtue. Since life underground might enslave his being as fully as hot buttered yams or ideological theory, it is no surprise that we hear from the hero's own lips that he must emerge.

Seeking to disclose an image of man *sub specie aeternatatis*,[1] the author of *Lord of the Flies* would surely agree with Reinhold Niebuhr that "man's inclination to injustice makes democracy necessary."[2] But because William Golding pictures history as the consequence of man's fall from essence into existence he has come under attack, from literary as well as political critics, for inviting a conservative, if not reactionary, vision of human potentiality. Looking beyond social action, writers like Golding, some argue, accept human injustice as a condition only God can remedy. By default, inaction becomes, at best, an apology for cynicism.[3]

The charge, generalized, opposes the notion of a modern, Christian hero. In this regard, Murray Krieger submits that this hero "ethically paralyzed" by virtue of human depravity, flees from the demonic to an "extra-ethical, subjective, existential Christianity."[4] Krieger confronts us with an important question: whether the Christian existentialist and, keeping *Lord of the Flies* in mind, his democratic counterpart, must withdraw from the contradictions of secular history to preserve faith.

While it is probably true that Protestantism from the time of the Enlightenment has tended toward a subjective notion of evangelism,[5] neither apocalyptic Christianity nor liberal democracy stress, by some historical or metaphysical necessity, inward change at the expense of social commitment. Indeed, under attack from a host of social and theological critics from Marx to Kierkegaard, Christianity has come progressively to affirm an existential quality of religious faith, grounded precisely in the type of interaction that characterized Reinhold Niebuhr's social commitment. In the words of Paul Abrecht, the modern theologians "plead for a new existential or contextual approach to replace the emphasis on theoretical norms or standards, and to put the focus on the discoveries of Christian community in the midst of the conflicts and tensions of society."[6]

Lord of the Flies reflects this important change in

religious consciousness. It should be viewed, moreover,
as a novel of social hope, dramatizing the hero's struggle to
preserve what an Aristotelian, a democrat, and a Maoist
revolutionary, as well as a Christian existentialist, might all
agree to be the true foundation of political action, namely,
human reciprocity.

From the first line of Golding's parable, when the
boy with fair hair breaks out of the undergrowth, to the final
description of him weeping for the loss of innocence, Ralph
achieves heroic stature by resisting the temptation to retreat
from the social and political realities that confront him. It
is neither through martyred flight from the destructive
realities of their island environment nor through a subjective
existentialism that *Lord of the Flies* offers an alternative
to despotism.[7]

The novel's action takes place on a deserted South
Sea island where some English schoolboys have crash-landed
during a future global war. Since no adults have survived, they
must protect themselves. Ralph, elected leader after the
remaining children have gathered together on the beach, is
aided in his task by Piggy and Simon (Golding's allegorical
representatives of reason and intuition). Their efforts
are opposed by Jack Merridew, the envious former choir
leader, who prefers hunting wild pigs to performing those
tasks that may facilitate their rescue. By offering a constant
supply of fresh meat and an exciting ritual surrounding
the hunt for food he entices the others away from the democratic society that Ralph, under the guidance of Piggy, has
created. On Castle Rock, Merridew establishes his totalitarian
regime, supported by a game-like ritual of self-effacement.
Masking their faces with paint, Jack's growing tribe of boys
turned savage defines itself orgiastically by sacrificing
slaughtered animals to a mythical "beastie." The chanting
circle which the hunters form around each pig offers initiates
tribal protection from the distress of their isolation. While
Ralph opposes this disinclination to be free, like the others he

Ralph

is tempted to join the dance which soon turns its passion toward human victims; when he and Piggy succumb momentarily to their own desire for forgetfulness, they participate in the orgiastic murder of their friend Simon. Finally, after Piggy's brutal death, Ralph remains the last hope for community on the formerly idyllic island. He is saved from becoming the tribe's victim by the sudden intrusion of an adult rescuer.

When an escape tube first jettisons the boys from their damaged plane, they fall into a tropical paradise. An improvement upon the legendary garden, this unnamed Eden needs no cultivating. A plentiful supply of food, protective foliage and countless possibilities for diversion all offer them an interlude from the desolation of atomic war. With only the tasks of building shelters and keeping a signal fire burning to qualify self-indulgence, the boys soon create a sordid replica of the holocaust from which they have come and to which, by grace of a British cruiser, they ultimately return. The children's metamorphosis from innocence to bestiality reflects Golding's sense of Biblical sin: like Adam and Eve, they cannot sustain innocence;[8] experience would appear to contribute the motivation for self-destruction. Since the small community depends for rescue upon an adult world by all indications in the process of atomic annihilation, the general failure to maintain hope seems ironically justified.

Ralph's responsibilities as leader force him to confront prematurely those considerations that undermine the will to affirm meaning. His questions, probing human contradiction, rely ultimately on criteria whose validity is rarely mirrored in nature or, for that matter, in the model of adult behavior. Golding's cosmos is devoid of that sense of mystery Faulkner pictured in the wilderness. Behind custom lies an apparently unregenerative chaos. The character of each epiphany which the tropical landscape fosters in the imagination of its inhabitants varies with the viewer. "If faces were different when lit from above or below," Ralph speculates sadly while watching the sun, "what was a face? What was anything?"[9] In the course of his tragic education Golding's hero learns, like King Lear, to improvise.

While Ralph's disenchantment largely follows his unhappy sophistication, Golding qualifies the magic of the children's new environment even before his hero realizes the wearisomeness of life. Ralph's enraptured surprise over the inviting pool of water, whose crystal clear bottom sparkles with tropical weeds and coral, leads him initially to speculate whether such natural beauty was the work of God, some typhoon, or the storm that had accompanied him to the island. The coral reef, facing the pool, appears "scribbled in the sea as though a giant had bent down to reproduce the shape of the island in a flowing, chalk line but tired before he had finished" (p. 30). Golding establishes the absurdly fortuitous character of natural phenomena as one of his important themes and continues to undercut the paradisiacal aspect of the island's typography. As Ralph observes his new world, he sees "a bank covered with coarse grass, torn everywhere by the upheavals of fallen trees, scattered with decaying coconuts and palm saplings" (p. 6). The forest itself appears ominously dark, while around and beyond the coral reef the "brute obtuseness of the ocean" engulfs his hopes for rescue. Although the palm trees supply abundant fruit for the abandoned children, the booming sound of insects rising from these ripe groves qualifies the reader's delight. Edgar's stark words in *King Lear* ("Ripeness is all") convey the dread that pervades this fecund world. No moral impulse emanates from its tropical foliage to instruct in proportion and moderation. The island speaks rather of a wideness wherein everything is permitted.

The novelist's use of children compares with Wordsworth's intentions in the *Lyrical Ballads*. Both seek to portray "the essential passions of the heart" in primitive simplicity. Golding's parable magnifies the infantile source of those universal fears that drive man to exchange his

dreadful freedom for a stabilizing idolatry. It is chiefly the
children's need for someone to order and direct their lives that
sustains Merridew's despotism. *Lord of the Flies*, however,
does more than document man's natural depravity; through
Ralph, the absurd determination to oppose nihilism with
"care" emerges as no less indigenous to man's historical being.

But what motivates care? Piggy cares about
returning to adult society because it offers him an automatic
and fully constituted authority. He assumes that if the
boys can be made to perform the principal task necessary for
rescue, maintaining the signal fire, the meaning of life will
be preserved. Although in one respect he is right, Piggy
never questions the validity of this derived meaning. His reason
for wanting to survive is disclosed when he tells Ralph:
"That's what grown-ups would do." On the other hand,
Simon's concern over man's depravity drives him ultimately
to renounce the self capable of responsible action; as in
Septimus' martyrdom, he chooses to withdraw from a world
where evil is inevitably present.

Martin Heidegger (and Sartre expresses a similar
idea) explains that "care" *(Sorge)* is motivated by the
individual's discovery that he alone is responsible for defining
his relationship to the world. Concern reflects man's anxiety
over doing the right thing and the realization that in any
case one must bear the consequences of his decision in regard
to other people. Heidegger's "everyday man" *(Das Man)*
dramatizes the universal temptation to forget responsibility
(Seinsvergessenheit) and thereby escape the anxiety of
guilt.[10] *Das Man*, aptly characterized by Fred Hale in *Brighton
Rock*, seeks the tranquillizing gift of anonymity.

Ralph fears his own desire to forget. "Supposing I
got like the others," he tells Piggy, "not caring. What 'ud
become of us?" (p. 167). The hero suffers because he recognizes his willingness to escape responsibility through the less
dangerous symptom of infantile regression ("be sucking
my thumb next" (p. 130), he speculates) and through his

crucial part in Simon's murder. No less than Piggy he is driven to hope that others will supply a remedy for the crisis on the island. "If only they could get a message to us," Ralph cries desperately. "If only they could send us something grown-up . . . a sign or something" (p. 109). Ironically, the only message the boys receive is through the dead body of a parachutist, an ominous reminder of what is happening outside, as well as the prop that serves to substantiate the children's imaginary "beastie." Ralph at times succumbs to the delusion that adult society is free of the evil he has recently experienced: "His mind skated to a consideration of a tamed town where savagery could not set foot. What could be safer than the bus centre with its lamps and wheels?" (p. 197). At these moments of self-deception the past offers Ralph relief from his sense of inadequacy. Like Sartre's anti-Semite, Ralph seeks to avoid his future by remaining passively dependent on a "good" that is already assumed.

Kierkegaard's statement, "It is only the lower natures which find in other people the law for their actions, which find the premises for their actions outside themselves,"[11] suggests the submission against which Ralph struggles. At the critical points of the hero's island existence he withstands the temptation to ground the premise of his life in another man's authority. This is as true of his relationship with Piggy and Simon as with Jack Merridew. Although Ralph's close friends grant him theoretical knowledge, they cannot lead him, as Virgil and Beatrice led Dante, out of darkness to Truth. In a post-Nietzschean age, emptied of God, reason and intuition exist like subjects without a ruler; both boys look to Ralph for the strength to survive. *Lord of the Flies* magnifies the absence of existential resolution in Piggy and Simon as well as the fanatical sadism of Jack and his hunters.

Piggy persists in looking outside himself for the reality as well as the value of his own existence. Both his need for attention and his compulsion "to do" suggest an often humorous unwillingness to be himself. While Piggy opposes the forces of nihilism by encouraging a policy of good works, he is essentially a comic figure. Quick to advise, but slow to participate in the effort or the pleasure of work and play, he defends his immobility on the grounds that "auntie" and asthma deny him all physical exertion. His literal reliance upon "grown-ups" in general and "auntie" in particular is a comic variation on the theme of man's effort to define himself through the identity that others allow him. At the children's first meeting Piggy contributes his nickname solely to gain attention; he feels compelled to choose a name that first satisfies the boys' urge to tease and finally their tragic need to destroy.

Piggy's total "other-directedness," reenacts the captivity of reason by bourgeois values.[12] The orphaned boy must create or discover a father to direct and sanction his activity. "Auntie," the complacent dispenser of middle-class sweetness and light (she owns a candy shop), indulges her nephew in a way that further hinders his independence.

If Piggy can find the man with the megaphone, if he can list all survivors, if an assembly can be organized, then something constructive will have been done. Golding expresses an alternative to this logic through Ralph during those first moments when his new friend urges him to action. Enraptured by the sight of the island—"Here at last was the imagined but never fully realized place leaping into real life"—Ralph faces Piggy's sensible plea: "We got to do something" (p. 13), with a smile of delight. While Ralph repeatedly obliges him, on this occasion Piggy mistakes his smile for a sign of recognition. Ralph, however, has responded with joy to a reality that his companion largely ignores. Golding would appear to honor Ralph's unstated question: why is it necessary to do anything? The hero's capacity to enjoy nature unfettered by routine is a precondition for his later successful confrontation with chaos.

The novel first describes Simon as "a slight, furtive boy whom no one knew, who kept to himself with an inner intensity of avoidance and secrecy." Sensing in particular the threat of other people, like Billy Budd he is inarticulate, at times insensible, before mankind's essential illness. As Merridew informs Ralph: "He's always throwing a faint" (pp. 20–21). The frail choirboy is most at home in the womb-like darkness of the matted underbrush where the creepers and bushes offer relief from the anxiety of a fallen world: "he left his sweat on them and they pulled together behind him" (p. 64). Fearing the crowd, Simon admires Ralph's ability to encounter the resistance of other people: "He sighed. Other people could stand up and speak to an assembly, apparently, without that dreadful feeling of the pressure of personality."

Ralph offers Simon as well as Piggy the gift of recognition. When he smiled at the timid choirboy, "for a moment or two Simon was happy to be accepted." His brief pleasure occurs, we are told, because "he ceased to think about himself" (pp. 121–122). Unfortunately, in this state of suspended subjectivity, he walks into a tree. Ralph becomes Simon's only point of contact with society; when Ralph joins the ring of savages during the storm, he unwittingly eliminates any possible historical reentry for Simon, who is murdered by all of his companions.

Simon contributes an understanding to Ralph that Piggy's reason is powerless to supply. Piggy greets Simon's suggestion that they climb the mountain to search for the beast "with an expression of derisive incomprehension" (p. 153): the confrontation either with evil or with death (expressions of the irrational) is unthinkable. Bewildered, he returns to the importance of tending the fire and of being rescued. Piggy shuns darkness and Simon flees from his own insight that life is a sickness unto death. The pig's head, with its host of flies, challenges Simon's unwillingness to face the strange evidence that destroys the security of his peace as surely as it disrupts the pattern of Piggy's reason. Once Simon has succumbed, his eyes cannot break away from the

severed head that Jack's hunters have hung on a stick to
appease the mythical beast. The head's grotesque incantation,
the projection of Simon's own inner knowledge of evil,
confirms the total isolation of the individual: "There isn't
anyone to help you. Only me." The Lord of the Flies fulfills
its dark prophecy with the words: "I'm part of you" (pp. 171–
172). But the assertion speaks to another part of Simon, the
"you" that may "try to escape," the "you" that is "not
wanted." Simon capitulates. Looking into the vast round aper-
ture, he experiences blackness that spreads about him. Drawn
into the mouth, he passively relinquishes consciousness.

When he awakens from the faint, his tragic knowledge has done more than qualify innocence. Simon is like
a man whose life is already over: "He walked drearily
between the trunks, his face empty of expression . . . The
usual brightness was gone from his eyes and he walked with a
sort of glum determination like an old man" (p. 174).
With the discovery of the form upon which the beast's reality
has been partially predicated—the dead parachutist left
decaying on the mountain—Simon starts down to inform the
others. But such news means little to children who have
posited the monster out of a need for something tangible.
Fear has supplied them an object more satisfying than
the obscure hope of rescue. Driven as they are by such
compulsion, their reaction to the news about the beast
is predictable. Simon, resigned to the futility of all "doing,"
perhaps senses this. If so, his descent from the mountain
reenacts his submission before the open mouth of the pig. The
empty ring of savages, including Piggy and Ralph, yawns
in expectation of its victim and, with Simon's murder,
the tribe's sacrifice to oblivion commences in deadly earnest.
Symbolically, the intuitive basis for hope has been removed by
an age in pursuit of forgetfulness. The description of
Simon's dead body moving silently out to sea, illuminated
by a sky full of constellations, glorifies the martyr's choice to
flee the world. But he gains peace at the expense of himself.

Six Existential Heroes

In an interview on the BBC, Golding called Simon
a saint because he "voluntarily embraces his fate." Later,
at Purdue University, the author agreed that his character was
also "a Christ figure." While Simon's many acts of
compassion apparently confirm these words, certain difficulties occur in Golding's treatment that may have emerged in
spite of his intention. In the New Testament, Simeon[13]
identifies Jesus as the child "set for the fall and rising again
of many in Israel." Significantly, it was revealed to him
that "he should not see death, before he had seen the Lord's
Christ." The fact that Golding's Simon, speaking "from a
higher rock," prophesies Ralph's rescue, shortly before his
own death, suggests an equal eminence for Ralph.

The nonhistorical character of sainthood that
Golding appears to hold complicates his attitude toward
Simon's obvious virtue. Although the interviews do not make
it entirely clear, Golding suggests that Simon's choice to
flee the world compares with Christ's surrender to Pontius
Pilate. The notion that Christ voluntarily embraces his
fate (Golding says this directly only about Simon) is questionable theology. The man Jesus was no more willing to be
crucified than was Socrates to be poisoned. Christ did not flee
society in the face of its unbending rejection of his beatitude.

Golding's understanding of Christ's martyrdom
need not concern us here. More pertinent is the apparent
distinction he makes between saint and tragic hero.[14] The
latter, unlike the former, suffers because he cannot transcend
history. He is committed to preserving his own existence
in a way that the martyr is not.

Simon and Piggy appeal to Golding; both stand as
alternatives to orgiastic despotism. If, as the novelist suggests,
man inhabits an absurd universe, then Piggy's optimistic
illusion that the operation of gadgets denies cosmologi-
cal absurdity and Simon's escape into the dark protection
first of the forest, then of eternity, is tragically justified.
As Kierkegaard's hero in *Fear and Trembling* fascinated his

narrator, however, so Ralph's heroic courage seems at times
to amaze the author who created him.

The fatigued gestures of Estragon removing a shoe
or studying a raw carrot while waiting for an ill-defined
and unreliable Godot are no less meaningful than the anxious
activity on the tropical island. In both cases absurdity is
humanized through the qualifying presence of those who
wait. Ralph, like Beckett's two tramps, joins in the dance of
life and death without weakening an existential eschatology
of hope. The Gospel of St. Luke first describes Simeon as
"waiting for the consolation of Israel"; Golding appears to
have developed this attribute chiefly in Ralph. At almost every
point, his quiet patience challenges both the tentativeness
of nature and the assertive tyranny of Merridew. This virtue
distinguishes the hero at once: "There was a stillness
about Ralph . . . that marked him out" (p. 22), a quality of
self-acceptance that requires neither sustaining arguments nor
self-approval. On the contrary, his life reveals an openness
to the experience that threatens his equilibrium. Unlike
Merridew ("One who knew his own mind," p. 20), Ralph
repeatedly looks beyond the intentions that define him
in the present. When he states to the assembly, "I said before
we'll be rescued sometime. We've just got to wait; that's all"
(p. 48), his words, like Graham Greene's description of
Rose running with passionate expectation through the stench
of her Brighton environment, reveal the hero's faith. The
questionable ends that motivate Ralph and Rose—in the first
case, return to an adult world incapable of avoiding war; in
the second, reunion with a teen-age killer—are less important
than their undeluded affirmation of hope in an absurd
universe. Consequently, at the moment of crisis, when objective uncertainty threatens to overwhelm them, Ralph can
still receive Simon's unreasoned prophecy, "You'll get back to
where you came from," and Rose can embody the old
priest's counsel to "hope and pray."

Since the existential hero is a part of the inauthenticity he perceives and repudiates, he must face the destructive propensities of his own subjectivity. Piggy denies the beastie; Simon flees from its historical consequences; Jack merges with it. Only Ralph survives in the courageous awareness of that perversity he shares with others.

After Simon's massacre, the island loses all vestige of innocent enchantment for Ralph. Unlike Piggy, however, he remains open to the experience of his own depravity. In the past, Piggy's logic has recalled his friend's memory to the task; now, in an atmosphere of futility, Ralph forces Piggy to remember what in fact occurred during the fateful storm: " 'That was murder.' 'You stop it!' said Piggy, shrilly. 'What good're you doing talking like that?' He jumped to his feet and stood over Ralph. 'It was dark. There was that—that bloody dance. There was lightning and thunder and rain. We was scared!' " Ralph denies the premise. His answer leads him to the important realization that within the circle of chanting boys he had ceased to exist as an individual capable even of fear, that he had surrendered to his own desire for nameless anonymity: "I wasn't scared . . . I was—I don't know what I was." The confession is confirmed by Golding's earlier suggestion that "Piggy and Ralph, under the threat of the sky, found themselves eager to take a place in this demented but partly secure society." Piggy, however, persists in rationalizing: " 'We was scared!' said Piggy excitedly. 'Anything might have happened. It wasn't—what you said.' He was gesticulating, searching for a formula." The formula he finally settles upon defines their inhuman act as an exception to the cosmic continuity that makes television sets work when you turn the switch and grownups appear when things get difficult. " 'It was an accident,' said Piggy suddenly, 'that's what it was. An accident' " (pp. 186–187).

Piggy's pragmatic arguments to deny their participation at the orgy lest the future (for him an extended past) call them to account for murder, is an invitation to forget their presence in the dance. "We was on the outside. We never done nothing, we never seen nothing" (p. 188). His suggestion that they can live on their own, apart from the others, assumes that evil can be localized and contained. When Piggy's rationalization that they are not responsible for evil tempts Ralph to forget his own complicity, the consequence is immediately apparent. That night, hearing sounds of movement outside the shelters, Ralph "prayed that the beast would prefer littluns." After the hunters attack the shelters, however, he regains his composure; he emerges from the fallen hut to reassure the younger children: "All you littluns, go to sleep. We've had a fight with the others. Now go to sleep" (pp. 199–200).

During the scuffle, Jack's tribe has stolen Piggy's glasses, which they need to start a fire to cook their meat. On their way to reclaim the glasses the next morning, Ralph and Piggy meet the others on Castle Rock, massed solidly together behind painted faces and wooden spears. Golding emphasizes the menacing chaos that surrounds the two boys. High above the savages' "incantation of hatred," one of them, "with a sense of delirious abandonment" (p. 216), leans his weight upon the boulder whose descent sweeps Piggy to his death. Below, the sea waits to suck all meaning into its formless depths. In Piggy it receives the savages' second offering to cosmic anarchy. Ralph, quiet and resolute, stands facing them. His courageous readiness to confront such odds with strength is no less absurd than Piggy's attempt to reason with the crowd. Ralph escapes only because the death of Piggy temporarily distracts the tribe's compulsion to destroy.

With the loss of his last friend, Ralph is on his own. From the time he flees Castle Rock to seek the protective covering of the forest until the final instant when the rescue that Simon prophesied does in fact occur, his struggle reaches its crisis. At first, like Piggy after Simon's death, he shuns the fatal and irrational facts of the recent murder: "No. They're not as bad as that. It was an accident." The atrocity

once conceived as an exceptional occurrence no longer
threatens society's foundation. Then, as Ralph rushes through
the thicket, he stumbles upon the pig's head still fixed upon
its pointed throne, the representation of evil's entrenched
presence in human nature.

Simon and Ralph confront the severed head in
radically different ways. The former, struggling to avoid
tragedy, keeps his face lowered, his hands shielding his closed
eyes from the medusa-like apparition. Only at the end does
he yield and look upon the beast; the knowledge of radical evil
brings on his faint. Ralph faces the peering skull with
characteristic openness. Golding's language emphasizes his
hero's willingness to see and oppose the satanic creation
of man's fear and the projection of his own destructive
inclinations. "He *saw* something standing in the centre . . . he
saw that the white face was bone. . . . He walked slowly into
the middle of the clearing and *looked steadily at the skull* . . .
[my italics] He stood, the skull about on a level with his face,
and held up his hair with two hands" (p. 221). When Ralph
finally backs away from the clearing after striking the skull,
unlike Simon, he keeps his eyes on the white and broken face.

Before the dangling head, as before the other boys,
Ralph's efforts appear absurdly out of place (in Sartre's
sense, *de trop*). He does not succumb, however, to its
inscrutable knowledge of evil—"The skull regarded Ralph
like one who knows all the answers and won't tell,"—but
takes the spear as a weapon with which to continue his
resistance. Fully awake in the growing darkness of night,
Ralph bears the anxiety of his isolation. The dread of
this experience strengthens the resolution necessary to endure
the worst horror of all, the stick sharpened at both ends that
Jack's hunters have prepared for him. Immediately Piggy's
former argument tempts him to hope that the others "would
let him alone; perhaps even make an outlaw of him." But
the "fatal unreasoning knowledge" of that darkness hanging
over the island denies Ralph the luxury of such fallacies. He

courageously perceives that his presence nourishes their
destructive identity, filling, like each sacrificial pig, the void
of the hunters' emptiness.

Earlier in the novel, the young hero confronts Jack's
hostility with the anxious question, "Why do you hate me?"
Receiving no answer, he soon asks Piggy to explain the
hatred that "makes things break up like they do." The latter,
more pleased to be accepted by Ralph than bothered by
the question, offers Jack—"It's him" (p. 167)—as the reason
for evil. While Ralph nods in solemn agreement, unlike
his companion he can understand the quality that drives
Merridew to hunt and destroy because he recognizes these
compulsions within his own nature. Consequently, as he
steps out of the clearing, the recurring sense of an undefinable
connection with the former choir leader is more than his
acknowledgment of Merridew's sadistic need to hunt him.
Ralph's sense of responsibility throughout the novel
encompasses the latter's despotism. Although he cannot
answer the question "Why?" he is aware and concerned over
what is really happening to Jack Merridew as well as what
is happening to himself.

Ralph preserves his solitary freedom against a world
striving to annihilate him and against his own compulsion
to forget that his resistance alone qualifies total chaos. In
flight, his greatest dread is that the curtain falling in his brain
may black out the consciousness of what is really happening
and make him like the others.

The soft darkness of the underbrush allows him the
same protection it had offered Simon. However, Ralph's
concern over preserving the future of his freedom
overshadows the momentary sense of peaceful liberation:
"One must remember to wake at first light." At daybreak
"he was awake before his eyes were open, listening to a noise
that was near" (p. 229). What follows is testimony to a fallen
world. As Ralph sadly perceives, his only crime was the
effort to keep a fire going, the sin of opposing nihilism with

care. His will to survive in the jungle against the advance
of Jack's army irrationally transcends both the futility of that
social mechanism he is committed to preserve and the
hopelessness of his continued rebellion. Although he might
escape their spears by bursting through the thin line of
savages, where is he to run? "The cordon would turn and
sweep again. Sooner or later he would have to sleep or eat
—and then he would awaken with hands clawing at him;
and the hunt would become a running down" (pp. 234–235).

Ralph's sense of being trapped by inescapable
forces bent on his destruction recalls a common motif in contemporary fiction. As Bigger Thomas leaps over the frozen
rooftops of his Chicago ghetto pursued by hostile and
insensitive white men, the thought of where he could go
drives the protagonist of *Native Son* to the realization that he
has been trapped since birth. The white man's rejection
of his humanity provokes Richard Wright's indictment of
the human race, an indictment from which Bigger himself is
not absolved. It is difficult to condemn this Negro turned
murderer for ceasing to care about anything.

The diminishing of alternatives confirms Ralph's
earlier experience of a world where "one was clamped down,
one was helpless, one was condemned." With the hunters
closing in on him, these alternatives race through his mind:
"Hide, break the line, climb a tree—which was the best
after all? The trouble was you only had one chance" (p. 237).
In an atmosphere of restrictiveness, Ralph's independence
emerges as political resistance. Dante at the end of his
pilgrimage no longer requires Virgil or Beatrice to guide his
responses. Similarly, Ralph's life now expresses a reason
and faith historicized through care and resolve. He has
translated the detached virtues personified in Piggy and Simon
into social action. But, even more important, this independence
includes a renewed sense of relationship. While his mind
perceives the consequence of the fire the savages have set
to smoke him out of the forest, his thoughts turn in concern to

their needs and their future as well as his own: "The fire must be almost at the fruit trees—what would they eat tomorrow?" No less significant is the voice within Ralph's consciousness, when all seems lost, repeating Simon's prophecy: "You'll get back" (p. 239).

Although the fire has virtually ended his resistance, as with Rose in *Brighton Rock* Ralph's hope survives to the last possible moment. His heroic refusal to forget extends to the final instant of his isolation. When the undefined adult form on the beach fills him with "hopeless fear," he recoups, prepared to resist new terrors.

Ironically, the savages' fire leads to rescue rather than destruction. Golding, whose conclusions often shock his readers' expectations (*Pincher Martin* is perhaps the best example), offers at the close of Ralph's struggle an absurdly improbable "happy ending." The method recalls Sartre's conclusion to "The Wall": Ibbieta's successful attempt to fool his Falange captors contributes to and reflects the cosmic anarchy that surrounds him. Fortune is neither a hostile force opposing man's worldly efforts nor a benevolent source of grace for the deserving. The accomplishment of Simon's prophecy is no less absurd than the prophecy itself.

More important than Ralph's good luck, his presence on the island has preserved the last vestige of democratic order. When the naval officer fortuitously appears, only Ralph has not relinquished his existence. "Who's boss here?" the officer demands. "I am," Ralph loudly asserts. Beside him the little Percival Wemys Madison, having forgotten everything about himself, can only stutter incoherently.

Ralph's filthy body, matted hair and unwiped nose do not distinguish him from the anonymous tribe of painted school boys. The polished captain turns away in embarrassment. The reader, however, experiences the unique character of Ralph's inner strength, the sad maturity that motivates his tears. While he weeps "for the end of innocence, the darkness of man's heart" and the death of his "wise friend called Piggy," his return to a conflagration of adult proportions, like Rose's return to the historicity of love's denial, cannot be construed as defeat. Through Ralph's courageous defense of personal freedom, William Golding would have us see that democratic community, however frail, may find new life.

Whether it is because Bernard Malamud is a Jew or simply because he is sensitive to the changes in American life that distinguished the sixties, *The Fixer* illustrates a growing political emphasis in the existential novel. Yakov Bok, like the heroes previously discussed, discovers himself by resisting the temptation to submit to the impositional intentions of others. He too chooses to endure suffering in the apocalyptic faith that his ordeal will prove meaningful. At the end of the book, however, he reflects on the most important insight his suffering has won: "One thing I've learned, he thought, there's no such thing as an unpolitical man, especially a Jew. You can't be one without the other, that's clear enough."[1]

Whereas *Lord of the Flies* might be set at almost any time in the course of Western civilization, the locale of *The Fixer*, Russia just prior to the first world war, is the precondition for Yakov Bok's emergence as a hero. Georg Lukács would surely approve. And yet, while the social environment of Kiev and the shtetl is central to Malamud's artistic intention, his novel invites a critique of Lukács's thesis that existentially oriented writers move necessarily toward an ahistorical form of romanticism.

Paul Tillich perhaps best describes the quality of existential historicity that Lukács finds objectionable. He clarifies the distinction between existentialism and essentialism in his *Systematic Theology:* "Existence is estrangement and not reconciliation; it is dehumanization and not the expression of essential humanity. It is the process in which man becomes a thing and ceases to be a person. History is not the divine self-manifestation but a series of unreconciled conflicts, threatening man with self-destruction. The existence of the individual is filled with anxiety and threatened by meaninglessness. With this description of man's predicament all existentialists agree and are therefore opposed to Hegel's essentialism. They feel that it is an attempt to hide the truth about man's actual state."[2] Tillich's words, as I shall suggest, illuminate Malamud's treatment of history. First, however, let us understand the basis of Lukács's objection to this type of analysis.

The literary expression of existential resignation, his argument goes, leads the best of modern writers to relinquish the concreteness of social history for "the ghostly aspect of reality."[3] Escapist literature, like all forms of psychological and linguistic positivism, presumes, he concludes, an unchanging, dogmatic view of human nature. At stake is man's capacity *to make* history through political action.[4]

Lukács speculates that in writers like Kierkegaard, the denial of unity between the inner and outer world leads necessarily to the isolation of man's inwardness. Threatened by cosmic absurdity, human personality comes to be identified more and more with an abstract subjectivity: "According to Kierkegaard, the individual exists within an opaque, impenetrable 'incognito.' "[5] In this sort of religious romanticism Lukács finds the seeds of a dangerous religiosity that ripens with Heidegger's glorification of Hitler.

To understand the motivation of writers like Kierkegaard and Malamud demands a distinction—one that Lukács is apparently unwilling to grant—between religious faith and the romantic quest for permanence. Ironically, it is precisely Kierkegaard's rejection of objective certainty implicit in all forms of dogmatism that motivates his religious faith. "The faith to doubt" describes Kierkegaard's intention here, and, if I am correct, Malamud's as well.[6] Consequently, authenticity remains for both writers a thoroughly imperfect achievement. This assumption clarifies Malamud's treatment of God and of value in *The Fixer*. The refusal of Kierkegaard and Malamud to sanctify their experience of estrangement— in Lukács's idiom their refusal to establish dogma out of the *condition humaine*—illustrates the distinction I wish to emphasize between existential and romantic heroism.

The Jewish-American novelist offers rich ground on which to explore this distinction. While writers like Bellow

and Malamud experience (as did Kierkegaard) the aesthetic
rewards of romantic self-pity, of creating a world bounded by
the limits of their own personal suffering, they resist the
appeal of *Weltschmertz*. Their heroes—Herzog, Morris Bober,
Yakov Bok—struggle against capitulation to inner as well as
outer compulsions that diminish growth. An inherent sense of
"incognito" leads them not outside history but rather to a
more Biblical sense of time and place.[7] We recall here the
qualities that drew Faulkner to the Old Testament: the concrete
faith of a people rooted in society and yet strangely
committed to a significance underlying all literal manifestations of deity.

    As I have suggested in discussing *Go Down, Moses*,
the Judaic conception of God lives in nameless mystery. This
notion of the divine beyond all human grasping yet "living"
in law and covenant posits an unacceptable contradiction
to many Marxists, unless mediated through some form of
Hegelian dialectic. To Christian and Jew, however, contradiction is a necessary paradox that accompanies the effort to
establish relationship between finite "I" and eternal "Thou,"
between existence and essence. Whether or not by
authorial intention, both the secular and overtly religious
heroes under discussion experience some aspect of this
paradox. The values that motivate their will to resist
inauthenticity may be derived, as Tillich has suggested,
from religious sources;[8] any such value, however, "exists"
through the hero's capacity to endure history.

    Yakov Bok is victimized through his own efforts to
escape the consequences of being a man, in Malamud's
idiom, of being a Jew. Deserted by his wife, Raisl, he has left
the shtetl for Kiev, determined to find better days. Living as
a Christian in a district forbidden to Jews, he finds himself
implicated in the alleged ritualistic murder of a Russian
school boy. During his long imprisonment, waiting for the
trial, the fixer comes to see his decision to leave the shtetl as a
denial both of himself and of history.

Although Yakov seems aware that the surrounding power structure of Russian society has deprived him of a humane standard of living, his response at the outset shuns action for rhetoric. He has good arguments and he uses them when talking with his father-in-law. "What can anybody do without capital?" he asks Shmuel with sustaining self-pity. The answer is: not much! "Opportunity here is born dead" (p. 7). Why then, the fixer asks himself, had he ignored his wife's plea to move from the shtetl? Looking back on the static nature of his past experience, Yakov blames the incapacity of body and spirit on his Jewish fate.

Like Shmuel, who owning almost nothing must sell his services, Yakov earns the barest living by fixing the broken ware of his impoverished community. When he finds work it is usually for nothing. The notion that he is more sinned against than sinning sustains him; drinking his tea unsweetened, the fixer gains more than the price of sugar: "it tasted bitter and he blamed existence" (p. 5). A Jewish Byron, Yakov's fatality is to live. Rhetoric is not the only means he finds for distraction: "Generally he moved faster than he had to, considering how little there was to do, but he was always doing something. After all, he was a fixer and had to keep his hands busy" (p. 9). His decision to move in many regards extends this need. Like an unlucky card player, he feels compelled to do something—"Change your place change your luck, people say" (p. 12). Without a basis for action, at least none grounded in his own ability to affect the course of events, Yakov finds that in leaving the shtetl for Kiev he has merely exchanged one prison for another. His choice to leave reflects the same captivity of spirit that held him rooted to the shtetl. More driven than driving, he does not experience the anticipated relief once on his journey, but, rather, "a deeper sense that he had had no choice about going than he wanted to admit" (p. 19).

From the opening sentence of Malamud's novel we are introduced through the fixer to a world in which the

motions of life reflect the absence of inner decision. Making
a living, in Yakov's terms, involves a pursuit of capital which
impugns his power to be moved inwardly. Not unaware of
this, he confesses early to Shmuel: "I fix what's broken—
except in the heart" (p. 7). His incapacity is symbolized on the
road to Kiev through the infuriating quiescence of the horse
Shmuel has sold him for the journey. His failure to force
movement from the unwilling creature conveys the physcho-
logical inability to project movement from within himself.

When the horse stands motionless, Yakov's dreams
"of good fortune, accomplishment, affluence" are diminished
by thought: "becalmed on the nag he thought blackly of his
father-in-law, beat the beast with his fist, and foresaw for
himself a useless future. Yakov pleaded with the animal
to make haste" (p. 24). Such a projected act of self-hatred
reveals the fixer's unconscious dependence upon those who
victimize him. After selling the horse—"He's only given
me trouble"—for fare to get across the Dnieper, he looks back
at the nag whinnying after them from the shore: "Like
an old Jew he looks, thought the fixer" (pp. 26–27). His new
self has not supplied an alternative that is any more than the
capitulation of existential preference. Even before the gates of
Kiev, it is the reality "that the ferry had stopped running
[that] sharpened the fixer's desire to get across the river."
And when the anti-Semitic boatman, finishing his violent
diatribe against the Jews with the hope that they will all be
annihilated, makes the sign of the cross, Yakov confesses that
he had to fight "an impulse to do the same" (p. 28). Like
Invisible Man, Malamud's hero is growing into the realization
that, driven by others, his life has been without a meaningful
center. And, as the opening of the second chapter suggests,
"Where do you go if you had been nowhere?" (p. 29).

Malamud's uprooted protagonists continually seek
forgetfulness through cultural metamorphosis. Fidelman
in "The Last Mohican" comes to Rome in the hope of
escaping his past failures: "He had read that here, under his

feet, were the ruins of Ancient Rome. It was an inspiring
business, he, Arthur Fidelman, after all, born a Bronx boy,
walking around in all this history."[9] The art student's
first sight of the Eternal City is interrupted by an itinerant
Israeli immigrant named Susskind who greets him with
—"shalom." "My first hello in Rome," mutters Fidelman,
"and it has to be a schnorrer."[10] In the course of this hilarious
tale, Fidelman finds that he cannot escape the schnorrer's
demand for charity without diminishing his own humanity.
Existence for the Jew, as for the Christian, remains a
communal relationship. When Susskind steals the first and
only chapter of his Giotto manuscript because Fidelman will
not give him an old suit, Fidelman finds his new life deprived of
a starting point. "He had tried writing the second chapter
from notes in his possession but it had come to nothing.
Always Fidelman needed something solid behind him before
he could advance."[11] It is, of course, the concreteness of his
Judaic past that his flight to Rome has sought to obliterate.

For Malamud, to deny one's own history is to
deny one's capacity for growth; it means to commit the self
necessarily to an abstract system of value that is distinct
from the existential dimension of human personality.
Fidelman's desire to be a critic of Renaissance art does not
spring from his passion to know Giotto and consequently to
explore new sources of creative energy. He seeks rather an
academic respectability that answers his need for distraction.

The appeal of other cultures, particularly the
exoticism of the unexperienced, is often an invitation for
romantic regression. This does not mean ideas cannot cross
cultures but rather that new ideas seldom eliminate the
environment they seek to affect. If Buddhism, for example,
were to appear as a transforming force in American religious
life, its authentic manifestation would have a distinctly
American inflection. The effort to leap out of one's historical
culture reveals for most existentialists a choice for self-
destruction. The self, formed always by the particularity of

its past, cannot escape the effects of its history. Being is rooted in time. To deny one's history is equivalent to denying one's self.

If Malamud's heroes often make the wrong choice, understood in terms of the preceding discussion, they initiate thereby a process that facilitates self-discovery. When Susskind steals Fidelman's manuscript, thereby disrupting his plans for an orderly year of scholarship, Fidelman is lost because he has nothing to do. He has not yet learned to make use of nothing. His culminating pursuit of Susskind reminds us of the comic flight of Invisible Man before the advance of Ras the exhorter. In both cases, insight occurs in the process of disruptive passion. In the case of Invisible Man it is fear; with Fidelman it is hatred. Although one is pursued and the other pursues, both discover themselves in relationship to the pursuer and the pursued. Their moment of self-realization is accompanied by a decision to stop running from others and from themselves.

Malamud's novel opens with the sight of people "running somewhere . . . everybody in the same direction." On the particular morning we hear "something bad has happened." The crowd's movement, we discover, is motivated by the news of ritual murder.

Hatred of the Jew throughout *The Fixer* appears in Sartrean terms. If anti-Semitism involves a choice, it is a choice without reflection. The picture of the Jew impressed upon the common man has been stamped there by church and state. Kogin, one of Yakov's more humane jailors, expresses the source of his mythology concerning Jewish "blood ritual" in the frankest terms: "I've heard about it ever since I was a small boy" (p. 233). In establishing the metaphysical principle that evil is localized in the Jew, leaders reap the political benefits of a scapegoat while encouraging an unreflective unity in the masses they seek to control. As I have suggested earlier, Sartre's *Anti-Semite and Jew* describes this inclination in every man as essentially anti-

intellectual. In bias, the anti-Semite finds the instant certainty
that reflection so easily dissipates. He chooses the sort of
static existence Lukács condemns. Running away continually
from any intimation of inwardness, his hatred of the Jew
becomes his compensatory need "to confuse [passion] with
personality." The motivating force in his bias is not hatred
of the Jew but a basic fear "of himself, of his own
consciousness, of his liberty, of his instincts, of his responsibilities, of solitariness, of change, of society, and of the
world."[12] So understood, his desperate movement is a movement without intention.

     While Sartre's words define the victimizers of Yakov,
they apply equally to the victim. The fixer's passivity reflects
society's more general disinclination to be free. Malamud
emphasizes his protagonist's willingness to be led in his
submission to the boatman and before his employer Nikolai
Maximovitch, as well as through his brief relationship
with the latter's crippled daughter. If his hesitation to yield
to Zina's seduction results from understandable caution,
it also represents Yakov's more general failure to make
history: "For himself he was willing to experience what there
was to experience. But let her lead" (p. 49). When she
suggests that they retire to her bedroom, he replies: "Whatever you say," prompting Zina to demand: "What do *you*
say, Yakov Ivanovitch?" (p. 51). We soon find that he hesitates
because of the thought she may be a virgin. Zina takes his
concern as a sign of old-fashioned morality. What Yakov
wishes is to avoid an involvement. "Should I stay or should
I go?" he speculates. His choice to live as a goy, to make a new
history for himself, is suddenly suspect. For the time
being he is neither goy nor Jew. Without intention, he is
still nowhere.

     If Yakov lacks the spirit to commit himself
wholeheartedly to one course of action or the other, the fault
is not solely his own. The fixer's neutrality arises from a
greater skepticism about the nature of life, both its depth

and its surface. As Kogin sums up his personal history—"You plan one thing and get another. Life plays no favorites and what's the use of hoping for it?" (p. 271). Kiev, that holiest of Russian cities, mirrors Yakov's soul as in a larger respect Malamud intends it to reflect the operative values of Western civilization. What is "holy" in Kiev, which is to say the ontological presuppositions of existence in Czarist Russia, are precisely those idols of the market place that have prompted philosophers as diverse as Bacon and Sartre to redefine human value. In this regard, we should recall the latter's assumption that existentialism is a humanism.

If freedom and movement do not mean the freedom to gain capital and security, what is left to hope for? Yakov's answer appears only too obvious. His life in prison, reduced by torture to the barest level of existence, is a living death. Understandably, the deepest wish throughout his ordeal is to be freed from this suffering. In the gentle and just Bibikov he finds a "potential savior" defending his "innocence" on the grounds of human law. Yakov at this time, relying on Russian justice, hopes he will be judged not guilty. But if free, what then? "He had pictured himself freed, hurrying back to the shtetl, or running off to America if he could raise the funds" (p. 182). Trusting in the very system of values that has led him to crisis, he continues, naively, to ignore Shmuel's historical insight that as Jews—"we live in the middle of our enemies." The urgency of Yakov's hope reaches a critical stage when he discovers the body of the prosecuting magistrate hanging dead in the adjoining cell. With Bibikov's murder, he has nowhere to turn: "Who would help him now, what could he hope for? Where Bibikov had lived in his mind was a hopeless hole . . . 'Mama-Papa,' he cried out, 'save me! Shmuel, Raisl—anybody—save me! Somebody save me!' " (p. 183).

Avoiding the existential act of self-affirmation, the fixer retreats once again to feverish activity. Walking in circles, he invents fantastic plans for escape, indulging himself in the pain of their impossibility: "He walked all day and into the night, until his shoes fell apart, and then walked in his bare feet on the lacerating floor. He walked in almost liquid heat with nowhere to go but his circular entrapment, striking himself on his journey—his chest, face, head, tearing his flesh, lamenting his life." The scene recalls an incident on the empty road to Kiev, when an old woman, kneeling before a large crucifix, repeatedly hit her head on the cold ground. The sight had given the fixer a headache, Malamud's humorous comment on his hero's psychological captivity. With metaphor become truth, self-mortification discloses another form of self-denial. In suffering for his innocence (he has done nothing) Yakov discovers his guilt: capable of neither love nor hate he is neutral. To resist, one must start from something; Yakov believes in nothing.

Opposition, while no foundation upon which to build social structure, is often the catalyst for existential growth. Lukács sets this principle in literary terms. Among the great heroes of fiction, he suggests, "it is just the opposition between a man and his environment that determines the development of his personality."[13] Without resistance man becomes a static extension of the environment that claims him by birth. In this light we understand why William Styron's Nat Turner must shake his fellow slaves from docile complicity into a realization of the white Southerner's uncompromising depravity before he can hope to initiate significant change. Echoing Bruno Bettelheim's experience of the Nazi concentration camp, Styron comments on the internal obstacles to self-liberation: "A Negro's most cherished possession is the drab, neutral cloak of anonymity he can manage to gather around himself, allowing him to merge faceless and nameless with the common swarm: impudence and misbehavior are, for obvious reasons, unwise, but equally so is the display of an uncommon distinction."[14]

"Neutrality" is an important word in *The Confessions of Nat Turner* and *The Fixer*. The protagonist of each

novel opposes his own inclination to take the course of
least resistance; like Ralph before Jack Merridew's painted
tribe, both withstand the temptation to merge with the
enemy. The notion of rebellion, like that of revolution, had
been anathema to the essentially apolitical Yakov. While he
admits early to Shmuel that by predilection he ought to be
a socialist, he confesses distaste for all forms of political
activism: "the truth of it is I dislike politics, though don't
ask me why. What good is it if you're not an activist? I guess
it's my nature." The fixer's retreat into philosophical
fatalism is another effort to avoid existential commitment.
Dismissing God—"A meshummed gives up one God for
another. I don't want either"—he allows an uncritical self-
interest to define his concerns: "We live in a world where the
clock ticks fast while he's on his timeless mountain staring in
space. He doesn't see us and he doesn't care. Today I want
my piece of bread, not in Paradise." Yakov's conception of the
Judaic God, ironically abstract, reveals his preference for
speculative resolutions: "I incline toward the philosophical"
(p. 17). Once he has been arrested for murder, however,
rationalization collapses. The picture that remains is one of
crawling subservience with neither dignity nor meaning.

Following the death of the prisoner Fetyukov, "shot
for disobeying orders and resisting a guard" (p. 184), the
fixer is lectured on the consequence of insubordination.
The instructions posted on the wall of his cell, like the demands
upon Invisible Man, instruct him in the ways of his world:
"Obey all rules and regulations without question" (p. 187).
The alternative is to face death. Stunned by the loss of
yet another individual who had shown him sympathy—
Fetyukov, though a Christian, had urged him not to lose hope
—Yakov submits. Unable to walk, he follows the warden's
command and crawls "like a dog" to the infirmary. Through
resistance, however, the uneducated peasant Fetyukov has
preserved the idea of opposition. His act stands in meaningful
contrast both to the fixer's temporary capitulation and to

Gronfein, the informer whose betrayal of Yakov arises
from a candid fear of death. Gronfein's submission to the
existing power structure holds a certain pragmatic validity.
Against such force all talk of heroism appears naively idealistic.

In the past, Yakov had been as casual about death
as he had been about life: "Death," he tells Shmuel, "is the
last of my worries" (p. 14). The deaths of Bibikov and
Fetyukov and Gronfein's arguments for survival threaten
his cultivated disinterest. Deprived of the means of doing
anything—"His hands ached of emptiness" (p. 201)—
and facing a charge that could result in his own execution, he
tries to find distraction in thought. Spinoza, whom he has
read most recently, comes readily to mind, but now it is not
philosophical principles he recollects but the picture of a
man like himself, denied by his own Jewish community,
who "died young, poor and persecuted, yet one of the freest
of men" (p. 207). The question of freedom recurs as the
fixer's thoughts turn to fragments of Psalms once memorized.
No longer safely abstract, the notion of God becomes an
image of himself "pursuing his enemies with God at his side,
but when he looked at God all he saw or heard was a loud
Ha Ha. It was his own imprisoned laughter" (p. 209). Yakov
cannot escape such implications.

When charged with revolutionary intentions,
however, he reverts once more to his former neutrality: "I
am not a revolutionist. I am an inexperienced man. Who knows
about such things? I am a fixer" (p. 226). We know this
is sham. Yakov is not a man without experience but, rather,
one who has sought to deny his own experience. Back in
his cell after the interview with Grubeshov, Yakov's personal
crisis reaches a peak as he identifies with his own victimizers
in one last orgy of self-effacement: "His fate nauseated
him. Escaping from the Pale he had at once been entrapped
in prison. From birth a black horse had followed him, a
Jewish nightmare. What was being a Jew but an everlasting
curse? He was sick of their history, destiny, blood guilt"

(p. 227). As he protests too much, his conversion is imminent.

Malamud's secular hero rediscovers the liberating depth of Judaic life through two unlikely sources, Spinoza and Jesus. His imprisonment reveals the historicity of Jesus in much the same manner as it had found in the life of Spinoza new possibilities for human freedom: "the story of Jesus fascinated him . . . he was deeply moved when he read how they spat on him and beat him with sticks; and how he hung on the cross at night. Jesus cried out help to God but God gave no help. There was a man crying out in anguish in the dark, but God was on the other side of his mountain . . . Christ died and they took him down. The fixer wiped his eyes" (p. 232). As in Styron's *Nat Turner*, God's absence paradoxically sparks religious faith.

Each of Yakov's pictures of God reflects stages of the hero's inner development. When trapped within himself, the fixer's image mirrored the reality of self-chosen solipsism. The widening of his sense of experience to include the being of others and the reality of time, past and present, results in an historicized image of God.

For history to begin, Israel must accept God's offer of covenant. Pursuing this insight, Yakov's thoughts lead him, like Kierkegaard, to consider God's existence as dependent upon man's willingness to respond. For God to be (in history), man must believe. God has chosen the Hebrews to preserve him, Yakov reasons: "He covenants, therefore he is" (p. 239). The historical reality of God involves the "experience" of God, for the Christian through Christ, for the Jew through covenant. In each case, the religious experience posits I and Thou. Here, the fixer's thinking, through its secular disposition, takes an interesting turn. Stressing the personal quality of Thou, his conception of God loses the perfection of an abstracted deity. When God is bound up with *zoon politikon*, his attributes take on the quality of phenomena ("things for us") as distinct from noumena ("things in themselves").[15] Such a God does not answer man's

need for escape. The resistance of bourgeois Christianity
to the idea of Jesus as a man with human needs and functions
suggests its desire to find in abstract ideality compensation for
the imperfection of existence.[16] Similarly, the secular as
well as the "religious" bourgeoisie have consistently sought
relief from the complexities of an industrialized society
through the worship of idealized heroes. The phenomenon of
hero worship in nineteenth and twentieth century Western
society, apparent at every level of the social scale, reveals
impulses that shun history for romance.[17]

    The fixer's iconoclastic conception of an imperfect
God opposes all such idolatry. Yakov speculates that God
is so human, He may even envy man his humanness: "Maybe
he would like to be human, it's possible, nobody knows"
(p. 240). His words recall Shmuel's earlier apologetic:
"Remember, if He's not perfect, neither are we" (p. 18). Out
of such imperfection, as I have suggested, arises the efficacy of
relationship. The God unaffected by the human condition,
appears, like Spinoza's abstract deity, on a timeless mountain,
an "eternal, infinite idea" careless of that which cannot
touch him. Experience cannot pull this conception of deity
from the realm of noumena to phenomena.

    The idea of an experiencing God leads to certain
difficulties. As a Jew, Yakov cannot posit an intermediary in
the form of Bibikov, Jesus, or Jaweh, and so he is confronted
once again with the question: How can an eternal God
"suffer" or "love"? With existential passion, Yakov reasons:
"If God's not a man he has to be" (p. 274). The acknowledgment that God and The Law depend upon his response
transforms the fixer's concept of experience. No longer
the passive recipient of luck or patronage, he begins to look
upon his life in terms of the history that has claimed him.
His identity, no longer conceived as an abstract potentiality,
moving through or standing aloof from historical events,
takes on new immediacy: "the experience was his; it was worse
than that, it was he. He was the experience." In realizing

that his existence is bound up with his suffering ("I suffer
therefore I am"), Yakov finds himself reunited with his past,
personified through Shmuel and Raisl. Resignation leads
him to a new maturity:[18] "I learned this but what good will it
do me? Will it open the prison doors? Will it allow me to
go out and take up my poor life again? Will it free me a little
once I am free? Or have I only learned to know what my
condition is—that the ocean is salty as you are drowning, and
though you knew it you are drowned? Still, it was better
than not knowing. A man had to learn, it was his nature"
(p. 316).

Were *The Fixer* to end here, it would portray
Lukács's conception of existential resolution. Malamud's
intention, however, is far from realized. As Yakov's
suffering increases following Shmuel's illegal visit, he
experiences a heightened sense of social responsibility.
Shmuel, for example, faces arrest as a consequence of his
involvement just as Bibikov paid with his life to uphold the
law through defending him. The fixer's new awareness has
won him more suffering. But now it is suffering *for* something
other than his own psychological liberation. " 'I'll live,' he
shouts in his cell, 'I'll wait, I'll come to my trial' " (p. 275).
No longer neutral, he sees that life involves reciprocity, that he
can suffer for others as well as for himself. The insight has
both tragic and political implications.

Kogin, we remember, despairs of meaning in the
world. His own cynicism regarding love mirrors the fixer's, for
both have seen the failure of all their plans. Our first sight
of the jailer anticipates his future actions and hints of his
role as Yakov's double. Outside the fixer's cell "he paced the
corridor as if he were the prisoner" (p. 190), his gaunt face
worn with the marks of worry. Listening to the Jew
reading about the trial and suffering of Jesus, he sighs with
sympathy; when his prisoner requests a small favor, a piece
of paper and pencil, Kogin does not return to hear him reading
the gospels. The reasons for his unwillingness to become

involved recalls Gronfein. "Don't think I am not aware of your misfortunes," he confesses, "but to be frank with you I don't allow myself to dwell on it much." If he helps the fixer, Kogin adds prophetically: "I could get myself shot" (p. 271).

His frankness about his own motives parallels the fixer's growing honesty about himself. While the jailer's service to his prisoner remains for the moment advisory—quoting the scriptural promise he has heard from Yakov's lips that "he who endures to the end will be saved" (p. 272)—Kogin soon perceives that to live this faith means to sacrifice safety and take sides against those who would deny man hope and justice. Intervening to save the fixer, he gives his life for the same principle that has motivated Yakov's endurance: " 'Hold on a minute, your honor,' said Kogin to the Deputy Warden. His deep voice broke. 'I've listened to this man night after night, I know his sorrows. Enough is enough, and anyway its time for his trial to begin' " (p. 326). His heroic resistance helps form the events that follow.

When Grubeshov first called Yakov an animal, the latter rebelled neither outwardly nor inwardly. Now, his decision to live, to come to his trial, accompanies the rage he experiences toward those who seek to dehumanize life. Facing Grubeshov's pharisaic judgment, he is no longer safely defensive: " 'And death is what you will get. It's on your head, Bok.' 'On yours,' said Yakov. 'And for what you did to Bibikov' " (p. 302).

Yakov's realization that the meaning of his life has expanded to include other people leads him to reconsider the reality of those external events that placed him in prison. Outside the shtetl, he has experienced the contradictions of living in a world where kindness is rewarded by suffering and reflection merely foresees complexity. "Who, for instance, *had* to go find Nikolai Maximovitch lying drunk in the snow and drag him home to start off an endless series of miserable events?" (p. 314). Stepping into history, however, *has* made a difference. An inner voice, in the image of Bibikov, professes Yakov's new sense of Being and time: "if you should ever manage to get out of prison, keep in mind that the purpose of freedom is to create it for others" (p. 319). In developing this insight, Malamud employs a metaphor that recurs with significant frequency in his fiction: "Once you leave you're out in the open; it rains and snows. It snows history, which means what happens to somebody starts in a web of events outside the personal. It starts of course before he gets there. We're all in history, that's sure, but some are more than others, Jews more than some. If it snows not everybody is out in it getting wet. He had been doused. He had to his painful surprise, stepped into history more deeply than others" (p. 314).

Snow, throughout Malamud's work, symbolizes the flux and possibility of history. Those who remain passive under the falling snow, like the evicted Kessler in "The Mourners," are doomed to a life without meaning. It is the great leveller of man's humanity. Under a common blanket of whiteness, Kessler's figure appears indistinguishable from the pieces of dispossessed goods that surround him. His failure to survive history represents his failure to love. Like Dante, who stands in the background of many of his works, Malamud characterizes the incapacity of mankind to love through figures of frozen immobility. Frank Alpine's name expresses the problem.

The discomfort of snow is not solved by moving to warmer climates. Malamud's characters continually face the temptation to flee the cold. Winter torments Helen in *The Assistant*: "She ran from it, hid in the house."[19] When she meets Frank Alpine in the public library (where she came often to escape the cold), the threat of intimacy frightens her. Walking home with him, under a cloudless sky, she hides her growing sense of vulnerability with a revealing non sequitur: "It feels like snow." What Helen dreads is the possibility that love will draw her into history. She shuns being out in the open where others (those who hate as well as those who love) may choose to involve themselves in her life and perhaps her death.

Snow, throughout *The Assistant*, points us toward an openness which includes life and death. Morris Bober dies as a result of clearing it from the sidewalk in front of his store, an act that paradoxically fulfills his need for a wideness he has not found in America:

> The spring snow moved Morris profoundly. He watched it falling, seeing in it scenes of his childhood, remembering things he thought he had forgotten. All morning he watched the shifting snow . . . he felt an irresistible thirst to be out in the open.
> "I think I will shovel snow," he told Ida at lunchtime.[20]

Frank Alpine, in choosing to make himself a Jew, preserves the old grocer's faith by taking up his burden. Again Malamud conveys the inspiration for this act through the metaphor of snow. The assistant has read a story about St. Francis in which the saint awakens one winter night with grave doubts about his religious life. Unable to sleep with the thought that he will never marry and have children like other people, he walks out into the snow. In an act of creative spontaneity the saint shapes a family out of snow, wife and children, then, kissing them, goes inside to sleep in peace. Frank, whose inner turmoil has continually led him to further acts of self-destruction, senses the significance of the tale.

Yakov's history begins when he sees Maximovitch half buried in the snow. At the close of the novel as he rides, through flurries of snow, toward his trial, he has learned to live in an imperfect world. Like Frank Alpine, his freedom is manifest in his choice to create order in a world of internal and external chaos. When an explosion wounds a cossack guard riding next to the carriage, the fixer is not immobilized

by the apparent absurdity of this incident. The wounded man,
his leg shattered by the bomb, looks through the window
at him, "in horror and anguish . . . as though to say 'What has
my foot got to do with it?' " (p. 331). No longer paralyzed
by his own guilt, Yakov's thoughts direct him to the heart
of the matter: The guard's suffering, like his own, is the
consequence of living in "the poorest and most reactionary
state in Europe" (p. 333). Conjuring a vision of Nicholas
the Second, Yakov charges the Tsar of Russia with responsibility for the failure.

   Malamud's final scene reveals the passive and self-
pitying Tsar as a projection of the fixer's former self.
Admitting that inequity exists in Russia, Nicholas defends
his own failure to act on fate: "I never wanted the crown,
it kept me from being my true self, but I was not permitted to
refuse." Like Yakov in the shtetl, his weakness reflects an
age that has lost faith in its own capacity to make history. The
Tsar's continual plea—"What can a man do . . . ? One is
born as he is born and that's all there is to it"—culminates
with a final disavowal of responsibility: "I am the victim, the
sufferer for my people. What will be will be" (pp. 333–334).

   A concentration camp such as Treblinka existed,
George Steiner suggests, "because some men have built it and
almost all other men let it be."[21] Yakov sees that neutrality
masks compliance, that in doing nothing Nicholas is equally
guilty. Raising his pistol, he shoots the Tsar (Russia's
"Little Father") dead. The act is a symbolic one. Like Invisible
Man, he is determined to be his own father. When Nicholas
asked him—"Are you a father?" the fixer replied—"With
all my heart," for he has taken responsibility for Raisl's
illegitimate child, as well as for his own deeper feelings. No
longer a fatalist, Yakov's last words, "Long live Revolution!
Long live liberty!" affirm his belief that there are ways
to reverse history. It remains to be seen, for Malamud as well
as for Golding and Ellison, if politics can ever be an expression
of love.

NOTES / INDEX

Notes

Introduction

1. Kierkegaard comes most readily to mind. H. Richard Niebuhr offers an interesting analysis, in this regard, of Kierkegaard's critique of culture: "Kierkegaardian existentialism gives up the culture problem as irrelevant to faith, not because it is existentialist and practical, but because it is individualistic and abstract; having abstracted the self from society as violently as any speculative philosopher ever abstracted the life of reason from his existence as a man. It abandons the social problem, not because it is insistent on the responsibility of the individual, but because it ignores the responsibility of the self to and for other selves." "Social Existentialism," in *Christ and Culture* (New York, Harper & Brothers, 1951), p. 244.

2. Jean-Paul Sartre, *Nausea,* trans. Lloyd Alexander (New York, New Directions, 1969), p. 134.

3. W. H. Auden, *For the Time Being* (London, Faber and Faber, 1945), p. 84.

4. In capitalizing the word "Being" I follow William Barrett's procedure, outlined in *What Is Existentialism?* (New York, Grove Press, 1964), pp. 136–137. Barrett discusses Heidegger's use of the verbal substantive "Being" *(Sein)* as it appears in the German philosopher's *Introduction to Metaphysics.*

5. *Nausea,* p. 175.

6. Iris Murdoch, *Sartre: Romantic Rationalist* (New Haven, Conn., Yale University Press, 1959), p. 3.

7. Ibid., p. 6.

8. Georg Lukács, *The Meaning of Contemporary Realism,* trans. from the German by John and Necke Mander (London, Merlin Press, 1963), p. 21.

9. Lukács's critique of modernism, as my chapter on *The Fixer* will suggest, helps to distinguish existential authenticity from romantic self-indulgence. Forsaking the reality of

contradiction that results once man conceives of his inwardness against the background of other people, the romantic modernist retreats into his own experience of solitariness and rebellion. By so doing, Lukács argues, his inwardness becomes necessarily more abstract, culminating often in a demoniac religiosity.

10. Jean-Paul Sartre, *Anti-Semite and Jew*, trans. G. J. Becker (New York, Schocken Books, 1968), pp. 17, 19.

11. Ibid., p. 18.

12. Martin Heidegger, "What Is Metaphysics?", *Existence and Being* (Chicago, Henry Regnery, 1949), pp. 347–349.

13. *For the Time Being*, pp. 114–115.

14. Murray Krieger, *The Tragic Vision* (New York, Holt, Rinehart and Winston, 1960), p. 13. While the encounter with nothingness has had its share of explicators, the tendency among critics of literature has been to treat both romantic and existential rebellion as an essentially demoniac advocacy. There are of course important exceptions, such as R. W. B. Lewis' *The Picaresque Saint* (Philadelphia, J. B. Lippincott, 1959), a study to which I am clearly indebted. Another important exception is Maurice Friedman's *Problematic Rebel* (New York, Random House, 1963). Friedman suggests that Job, by virtue of his deep trust in existence, "is the true existentialist" (p. 18). In contrast to Greek, Biblical, and Christian man, however, modern man remains a "rebel without a cause" (p. 54).

15. Søren Kierkegaard, *Fear and Trembling*, trans. Walter Lowrie, (Princeton, N. J., Princeton University Press, 1941), p. 48.

16. Through Johannes, Kierkegaard reveals the basis of his own incapacity to marry Regine Olsen. As the author confesses in his diary: "Had I had faith I should have remained with Regine." *The Journals of Søren Kierkegaard*, ed. Alexander Dru (London, Oxford University Press, 1951), p. 121.

17. Perhaps the most vivid example is Emile Zola's attack on romanticism as "a verbal construct built on nothing," *The Experimental Novel*, trans. B. V. Sherman (New York, Cassel Publishing Co., 1893), p. 65.

18. Charles H. Long discusses a new ontology based upon "language as a testimony to silence," in "Silence and Significance," *Myth and Symbols*, ed. J. M. Kitagawa and C. H. Long (Chicago, University of Chicago Press, 1969), p. 149.

19. Søren Kierkegaard, *Concluding Unscientific Postscript*, trans. David F. Swenson (Princeton, N. J., Princeton University Press, 1941), p. 267.

ONE / CLARISSA DALLOWAY

1. *A Writer's Diary*, ed. Leonard Woolf (New York, Harcourt Brace, 1954), p. 144.

2. For a good discussion of the historical background of this ontological shift, particularly the pre-Socratic Parmenides, see Paul Tillich's "Being and Nonbeing," *Systematic Theology*, vol. I (Chicago, University of Chicago Press, 1967), pp. 186–189. See also William Barrett, *Irrational Man* (New York, Doubleday, 1958), pp. 102–103.

3. Virginia Woolf, *Mrs. Dalloway* (New York, Harcourt Brace, 1925), p. 133, copyright, 1925, by Virginia Woolf; renewed 1953, by Leonard Woolf. Reprinted by permission of Harcourt Brace Jovanovich, Inc., the author's literary estate, and the Hogarth Press. All page references are to this edition.

4. While in this particular essay Virginia Woolf is dealing with the novelist's effort to portray character, her concern with that which makes a character seem real in fiction presumes and confronts a larger horizon of experienced reality.

5. Virginia Woolf, *The Captain's Death Bed* (New York, Harcourt Brace, 1950), p. 113. All page references are to this edition. The first version of her essay appeared in print in *Nation & Athenaeum*, December 1, 1923. The title of her Cambridge lecture was "Character and Fiction."

6. For an analysis of Heidegger's meaning here see William Barrett, *What Is Existentialism?* (New York, Grove Press, 1964), pp. 161, 185, and Magda King, *Heidegger's Philosophy* (New York, Macmillan, 1964), pp. 5–33.

7. *What Is Existentialism?*, pp. 141, 193.

8. Note Harvena Richter's discussion of the original working plan for *The Waves:* "The novel is visualized as a poetic-encyclopedic reconstruction of the creation and development of man and his mind, moving from his earliest awareness of objects—'the beginning with pure sensations,' Mrs. Woolf noted in an early outline of part one—to a perception of the world, death, and time." *Virginia Woolf: The Inward Voyage* (Princeton, N. J.,

Princeton University Press, 1970), p. 80.

9. Geoffrey H. Hartman speaks of "the affirmative impulse" in Virginia Woolf's critique of world as a quality of the artist that points dialectically beyond itself. *Beyond Formalism* (New Haven, Conn., Yale University Press, 1970), p. 74.

10. For a good discussion of the moment as a microcosm of Being in Virginia Woolf's writing, see Richter's *Virginia Woolf*, p. 40.

11. "Wittgenstein's Lecture on Ethics," *The Philosophical Review*, 74 (1965), 8–11.

12. In a letter dated July 28, 1965, Leonard Woolf informs me that although he and his wife did not know Wittgenstein well they spent some time with him when the philosopher stayed with Maynard Keynes in a house close to their own.

13. Martin Heidegger, "What Is Metaphysics?" *Existence and Being* (Chicago, Henry Regnery, 1949), pp. 325–361.

14. Hartman's discussion of "resistance" (in *To the Lighthouse*) helps clarify the struggle involved here. *Beyond Formalism*, p. 73.

15. "What is Metaphysics?", p. 336.

16. One of Sigmund Freud's late comments on the artist, quoted by Ernest Jones, seems particularly relevant: "The artist, like the neurotic, had withdrawn from an unsatisfying reality into this world of imagination; but, unlike the neurotic, he knew how to find a way back from it and once more to get a firm foothold in reality." *The Life and Work of Sigmund Freud*, vol. III (New York, Basic Books, 1957), p. 421.

17. *Writer's Diary*, p. 46.

18. Ibid., p. 61.

19. John Graham, in his fine article, "Time in the Novels of Virginia Woolf," *University of Toronto Quarterly*, 18 (January 1949), discusses Clarissa's return to the party in terms of her capacity to conquer time, pp. 189–190.

20. Martin Heidegger's discussion of "the temporality of resoluteness" and the manner in which "a moment of vision . . . makes the situation authentically present," serves as an illuminating gloss on the closing section of the novel. *Being and Time*, trans. John Macquarrie and Edward Robinson (New York, Harper & Row, 1962), p. 463.

TWO / ROSE WILSON

1. The first American edition, published by Viking Press in 1938, was listed as an "entertainment."

2. Graham Greene, *Brighton Rock*, copyright 1938, 1966 by Graham Greene. Reprinted by permission of the Viking Press, Inc., William Heinemann, and the Bodley Head. (London, William Heinemann and the Bodley Head, 1955), p. 44. All page references are to this edition.

3. A. A. De Vitis has emphasized that "to understand *Brighton Rock*, it must be read much as a medieval allegory." "Allegory in 'Brighton Rock,' " *Modern Fiction Studies*, 3 (1957), 219.

4. Robert O. Evans discusses a similarity in the thought of Greene and Sartre in his essay "Existentialism in Greene's 'The Quiet American,' " *MFS*, 3 (1957), 241–248.

5. In this sense, Herbert R. Haber states that "none of Greene's heroes ever reach spirituality by following the rules." "The Two Worlds of Graham Greene," *MFS*, 3 (1957), 257.

6. As De Vitis explains: "This is the worst horror of all, that Rose must return to life; life without hope, world without end" (p. 224). I believe, however, that Rose's presence, tenuous as it may be, qualifies the evil that encompasses the world at the close of the book.

7. Sean O'Faolain, *The Vanishing Hero* (London, Eyre & Spottiswoode, 1956), p. 86.

8. In fairness it should be noted that Greene, as part author of the script, evidently supported the change. As John A. V. Burke suggests in describing the end of the film: "The author connived by agreement with the vandalism his magnificent story thus suffered." "Signs of a Renaissance," *Sight and Sound*, 17 (Winter 1948), 175.

9. R. W. B. Lewis suggests that the film's ending reveals rather "the mixture of loathing and attraction which is Pinkie's real and bewildered attitude to Rose." "The 'Trilogy' of Graham Greene," *MFS*, 3 (1957), 199 n.

10. Murray Krieger, *The Tragic Vision* (New York, Holt, Rinehart and Winston, 1960), p. 266.

11. In *Another Mexico*, Greene wrote: "Faith came to one —shapelessly, without dogma." His words help define Rose's life.

12. Martin Buber, *I and Thou* (New York, Charles
Scribner's Sons, 1958), p. 9.

THREE / ISAAC McCASLIN

1. Jean-Paul Sartre, *Literary Essays* (New York, Wisdom
Library, 1957), p. 82.
2. For a discussion of Faulkner's influence on Sartre, see
Malcolm Cowley, *The Faulkner-Cowley File* (New York, Viking
Press, 1966), pp. 24, 87.
3. *Cowley File,* pp. 112–113. For an opposing view see
Marvin Klotz, "Procrustean Revision in Faulkner's 'Go Down,
Moses,' " *American Literature,* 37 (March 1965), 1–16.
4. See Faulkner's comments on *Absalom, Absalom!*
and Second Samuel, *Faulkner in the University,* ed. F. L. Gwynn and
J. L. Blotner (Charlottesville, University of Virginia Press, 1959),
p. 76.
5. William Barrett, *Irrational Man* (New York,
Doubleday, 1958). See particularly pp. 68–69.
6. William Faulkner, *Go Down, Moses* (New York,
Random House Modern Library, 1955), p. 163. Reprinted by
permission of Random House. All page references are to this edition.
7. While we find this idea chiefly in Heidegger's later
work, it appears earlier. See for example *Being and Time* (New York,
Harper & Row, 1962), p. 463.
8. The art historian Roger Fry suggests in *Vision and
Design* (New York, Brentano's, 1924), pp. 24–25, that each of us
learns to see only so much as our purposes require, which is
"just enough to recognize and identify each object or person." He
adds that "it is only when an object exists *in our lives* [my italics]
for no other purpose than to be seen that we really look at it."
Although his pronouncement is chiefly an indictment of the British
public's self-righteous condemnation of the French impressionist
painters (they have seldom looked at the nature whose "untruth"
they criticize in Monet), Fry raises the more difficult question of how
we can learn to see something that exists outside our frame of
reference. Is not all seeing in this regard a subtle form of
appropriation?
9. *Faulkner in the University,* p. 161.

148

10. The photographer-protagonist of Michelangelo Antonioni's film *Blowup* may be said to illustrate a similar passion to fathom experience.

11. Paul Tillich, rejecting the conception of a purely spatial "history" by which one derives the beginning, middle, and end of an extended period of time, argues that it is the point in which history reveals its meaning that is decisive: "History is constituted . . . by the fact that a center proves to be a center through creating history . . . Beginning is the event in which the genesis of that development is seen, for which the center has constituted itself a center." *The Interpretation of History* (New York, Scribners, 1936), pp. 249–250.

12. See John Lydenberg's "Nature Myth in Faulkner's 'The Bear,'" *American Literature*, 24 (March 1952), 56–72, for a discussion of this theme.

13. For a fuller discussion of this moment see R. W. B. Lewis, "The Hero in the New World," *Kenyon Review*, 13 (Autumn 1951), 641–660.

14. *Faulkner in the University*, p. 167.

15. In this regard, it is interesting to note Keats's definition of "World" as "Elemental Space." "To the George Keatses," April 1819, *The Letters of John Keats, 1814–1821*, ed. H. E. Rollins (Cambridge, Harvard University Press, 1958), vol. II, p. 102.

16. Albert Camus, *The Stranger*, trans. Stuart Gilbert (New York, Alfred A. Knopf, 1953), p. 76.

17. Ibid., p. 153.

18. Paul Tillich, *The Courage to Be* (New Haven, Conn., Yale University Press, 1956), p. 17.

19. In Leviticus 23:23 the ram's horn announces the new year and the new kings; in Psalm 47 the God of Abraham is proclaimed; and in Numbers 10 Moses, following God's instructions, makes two silver trumpets to be blown both in gladness and in sorrow, as "an ordinance forever throughout your generations." The narrator of Psalm 22 cries out for God to hear him as the Lord has heard him in the past through the horn of the "wild oxen." For the latter the new translation of the Bible substitutes the more accurate designation "unicorn."

FOUR / INVISIBLE MAN

1. Ralph Ellison, *Shadow and Act* (New York, Random House, 1964), p. 179.

2. Ralph Ellison, *Invisible Man* (New York, Random House, 1952), pp. 27–29. Reprinted by permission of Random House. All page references are to this edition.

3. The assumption characterizes Ellison's literary argument with Irving Howe. The debate is available most conveniently in Ellison's "The World and the Jug," *Shadow and Act*, pp. 107–143, and in Howe's "Black Boys and Native Sons," *A World More Attractive* (New York, Horizon Press, 1963), pp. 98–122.

4. *Shadow and Act*, p. 57.

5. Paul Tillich highlights this human propensity in discussing the fundamental, existential question: Why is there something; why not nothing? "Looked at from the standpoint of possible nonbeing, being is a mystery. Man is able to take this standpoint because he is free to transcend every given reality. He is not bound to beingness'; he can envisage nothingness; he can ask the ontological question." *Systematic Theology*, vol. I (Chicago, University of Chicago Press, 1967), p. 186.

6. *The Journals of Soren Kierkegaard*, ed. Alexander Dru (London, Oxford University Press, 1951), p. 372.

7. This suspension of intent reflects Ellison's idea of the experimental nature of art and, more particularly, the novel. See "Society, Morality, and the Novel," *The Living Novel: A Symposium*, ed. Granville Hicks (New York, Macmillan, 1957), pp. 58–91.

8. Ellison employs a number of Christian themes in treating his protagonist's mountain eulogy. Invisibility is a central motif in Matthew 5 and 6. Although good deeds as well as Godhead remain unseen, it is those with no possessions (with no things) that paradoxically "shall see God." The sermon on the mount urges man to commit himself to the hallowed *name* of Father, whose kingdom, power, and glory are present only through faith. When the object of faith becomes visible to man, the end of history will signify the arrival of the millennium.

9. *Shadow and Act*, p. 147.

10. Marcus Klein, *After Alienation* (New York, World Publishing Co., 1964), p. 134.

11. *The Living Novel*, p. 76.

12. Kierkegaard's knight of faith chooses, without self-deception, to believe in the possibility of the impossible.

FIVE / RALPH

1. William Golding, "The Writer in His Age," *The London Magazine*, 4 (May 1957), 45.

2. Reinhold Niebuhr, *The Children of Light and the Children of Darkness* (London, Nisbet, 1945), p. vi.

3. Bruce Franklin, "The Teaching of Literature in the Highest Academies of the Empire," *College English*, 31 (March 1970), pp. 556–557. From a nonradical perspective Francis E. Kearns in "Golding Revisited," *Lord of the Flies: A Source Book* (New York, Odyssey Press, 1963), p. 169, suggests that "college students acclaim *Lord of the Flies* for the same reason that they acclaim the novels of Ayn Rand.".

4. Murray Krieger, *The Tragic Vision* (New York, Holt, Rinehart and Winston, 1960), p. 266.

5. Robert McAfee Brown, *The Spirit of Protestantism* (New York, Oxford University Press, 1961). See particularly pp. 202–205.

6. Paul Abrecht, "The Development of Ecumenical Social Ethics," *Christian Social Ethics in a Changing World*, ed. J. C. Bennett (New York, SCM Press, 1966), p. 162.

7. Neither is Ralph's alternative an ironic rebellion motivated by futility. This type of ironic hero is discussed by Charles I. Glicksberg in *The Tragic Vision in Twentieth Century Literature* (Carbondale, Southern Illinois University Press, 1963).

8. In this regard, I disagree with Samuel Hynes's assumption that innocence has *existed* for Ralph *only* (my italics) "as an illusion made of his own ignorance." *Columbia Essays on Modern Writers, 2: William Golding* (New York, Columbia University Press, 1964), p. 15.

9. William Golding, *Lord of the Flies*, copyright 1954 by William Gerald Golding (New York, Coward-McCann, 1962), p. 89. Reprinted by permission of Coward-McCann & Geoghegan,

Inc., and of Faber and Faber Ltd. All page references are to this edition.

10. Martin Heidegger, *Being and Time* (New York, Harper & Row, 1962), pp. 163–168.

11. Søren Kierkegaard, *Fear and Trembling* (Princeton, N. J., Princeton University Press, 1941), p. 63.

12. For a good discussion of Golding's symbolic intentions see Hynes's *William Golding*, pp. 5–6.

13. It perhaps should be pointed out here that Simon and Simeon are orthographic variants of the same name. George M. Wilson has suggested to me that both Simon Peter and the Simeon of Luke 2:25 identify and announce Jesus's true vocation. One can see attributes of both New Testament figures in Golding's characterization of Simon.

14. Louis L. Martz, "The Saint as Tragic Hero," *Tragic Themes in Western Literature* (New Haven, Conn., Yale University Press, 1956), pp. 150–177, helps clarify this distinction.

SIX / YAKOV BOK

1. Bernard Malamud, *The Fixer*, copyright 1966 by Bernard Malamud (New York, Farrar, Straus and Giroux, 1966), p. 335. Reprinted by permission of Farrar, Straus & Giroux, Inc. All page references are to this edition.

2. Paul Tillich, *Systematic Theology*, vol. II (Chicago, University of Chicago Press, 1967), p. 25. Tillich's response to the question of whether he regarded himself as an existentialist was often equivocal. At Stanford in 1965 he replied: "Fifty-fifty."

3. Georg Lukács, *The Meaning of Contemporary Realism* (London, Merlin Press, 1963), p. 25.

4. For a discussion of this idea see George Lichtheim, *George Lukács* (New York, Viking Press, 1970), pp. 52–53.

5. *Contemporary Realism*, p. 27. From a theological perspective, Rubem A. Alves in *A Theology of Human Hope* (Washington, D. C., Corpus Books, 1969), while acknowledging that "existentialism has a great affinity with political humanism" (p. 34), describes Kierkegaard as one whose "thought moves in the sphere of a radical asceticism regarding everything that means time

or objective" (p. 36). Like Lukács, Alves considers Kierkegaard's thought essentially ahistorical.

6. The phrase is the title of M. Holmes Hartshorne's *The Faith to Doubt* (Englewood Cliffs, N. J., Prentice-Hall, 1963).

7. The distinction William Barrett makes between Hebraism and Hellenism is relevant here. *Irrational Man* (New York, Doubleday, 1958), chap. IV.

8. *Systematic Theology*, vol. II, pp. 25–26.

9. Bernard Malamud, *The Magic Barrel* (New York, Farrar, Straus & Cudahy, 1953), p. 162.

10. Ibid., p. 157.

11. Ibid., p. 172.

12. Jean-Paul Sartre, *Anti-Semite and Jew*, trans. G. J. Becker (New York, Schocken Books, 1968), pp. 52–53.

13. *Contemporary Realism*, p. 28.

14. William Styron, *The Confessions of Nat Turner* (New York, Random House, 1967), p. 65.

15. Lichtheim, pp. 58–59: Lichtheim suggests that all forms of positivism, from the realism of the scholastics to the presuppositions of social and natural science, tend to ignore this distinction.

16. The pursuit of such transcendence wherein all human contradiction is mediated and existence stripped of contingency often claims a transhistorical, "religious" intention. Deprived of history, the holy finds its only sanction in a world above the world. For a discussion of the Greek character of this assumption see Tom F. Driver, *The Sense of History in Greek and Shakespearean Drama* (New York, Columbia University Press, 1960). Thorleif Boman, *Hebrew Thought Compared with Greek* (New York, W. W. Norton, 1970) also develops some relevant distinctions here.

17. A recent example of the need for charismatic leadership is found in the attack of ten black writers on Styron's *Nat Turner*. Indicting Styron for creating a neurotic protagonist, replete with white America's "hang-ups," these critics largely refuse to see the historical Nat Turner in anything but idealistic terms. Eugene D. Genovese's review of *Ten Black Writers Respond*, *The New York Review of Books*, September 12, 1968, p. 34, makes the

following point: "those who look to history to provide glorious moments and heroes invariably are betrayed into making catastrophic errors of political judgment. Specifically, revolutionaries do not need Nat Turner as a saint; they do need the historical truth of the Nat Turner revolt, its strength and its weakness."

18. Eric Levy develops this idea of historical redemption in a 1971 Stanford Ph.D. thesis. Ihab Hassan suggests, on the other hand, that the widespread presence of revulsion in modern thought "is a confession that man finds no redemption in history." *Radical Innocence* (Princeton, N. J., Princeton University Press, 1961), p. 13.

19. Bernard Malamud, *The Assistant* (New York, Farrar, Straus and Cudahy, 1957), p. 88.

20. Ibid., p. 221.

21. George Steiner, *Language and Silence* (New York, Atheneum, 1967), p. 156.

INDEX

In this index 86f means separate references on pp. 86 and 87, 86ff means separate references on pp. 86, 87, and 88; 86–88 means a continuous discussion. *Passim*, meaning "here and there," is used for a cluster of references in close but not consecutive sequence (for example, 86, 87, 89, 90, 93 would be written as 86–93 *passim*).

Index

Index

Index

Index

Index

Index